From the library of

_____

GIVING FOR GROWTH

Achieving Success Through Giving Back

Jeremy C. Park

GIVING FOR GROWTH

Achieving Success
Through Giving Back

Foreword by Johnny Pitts

"The American way of life is under fire. Children born into poverty are less likely to rise than a generation ago. New business formation is trending downward. Capitalism is in danger of losing its broad appeal. Jeremy Park of cityCURRENT and Lipscomb & Pitts shows how to reverse these trends. Park reveals a timeless truth, once said by *Forbes* Magazine founder, B.C. Forbes: 'The purpose of business is to produce happiness, not pile up money.' *Giving for Growth* is the way forward."

Rich Karlgaard, Publisher/Columnist,
***Forbes* Magazine**

"Jeremy Park is certainly an expert on giving. Both his life AND his life's work exemplify the giving back of one's time, talent and treasure. In *Giving for Growth*, he taps into one of life's paradoxes – the more we give, the more we get. Surely the more we cling to, the bigger our pile gets, right? But God intended for us to be givers in order to experience all that life has for us. Only once does God ever encourage us to test him to prove one of his promises. 'Give and see if I will not open the windows of heaven and pour out a blessing such that you will not have room to contain it.' (Malachi 3:10). *Giving for Growth* provides inspirational and practical examples of how giving leads to growth. Measurable growth in our businesses. Personal growth for our employees. Growth in our communities. And maybe most importantly, personal growth and satisfaction."

Robert B. Carter, Executive Vice President
FedEx Information Services and CIO of FedEx Corporation

"Whether it's in business or government, people want to deal with folks who they know are committed to the greater good. *Giving for Growth* is about the wisdom of lending a helping hand to be a part of the greater good. Along the way, relationships are formed as people seek to meet the needs that surround them. The trick is in not being overwhelmed by the need and instead, creating small actionable steps so that everyone can help. I think this book can be a guide on how to do that."

Bill Haslam,
Governor of Tennessee

"*Giving for Growth* will INSPIRE you to BELIEVE that ANYTHING is POSSIBLE in your life, career, and BELOVED community! Jeremy's insight will allow you to ACHIEVE SUCCESS by better leveraging your GIFTS and PLATFORM to IMPACT others and create PHILANTHROPIC IMPRESSIONS that will LIVE FOREVER as your LEGACY. This book will challenge your thinking on how community CHANGE can be created and provide you the tools to become a CATALYST that uplifts HUMANITY and lives a LIFE FULFILLED!"

**Dr. Manny Ohonme, Founder, President and CEO,
Samaritan's Feet International**

"*Giving for Growth* brings into focus a simple reality, that relationships matter in every aspect of our lives and community. Jeremy does a wonderful job of articulating why giving of ourselves, our time, resources and expertise helps build not only a better community, but a better world one relationship at a time. You'll be inspired to reach out, help and make a difference. In return, you'll recognize that living a life with purpose is why we're all here, a realization that provides the foundation of relationships essential to hope and happiness."

**Dr. M. David Rudd, President
University of Memphis**

"Jeremy C. Park is a true philanthropist: he loves people, and in *Giving for Growth*, he uses powerful stories to show how philanthropy benefits everyone, including the givers themselves. Whether you lead an established non-profit organization or just want to make a positive difference in your own community, the simple but powerful guidelines in this essential work will show you how to give gifts that keep on giving."

**Bruce Weinstein, Ph.D., The Ethics Guy®,
Author, *The Good Ones: Ten Crucial Qualities
of High-Character People.***

"*In Giving for Growth*, Park offers the reader three truths, that when utilized, lead to a more meaningful and fulfilled life for both the reader and for those the reader seeks to lead, affirm, serve, and/ or love. What makes these aptly arraigned truths most poignant is Park's understanding and explanation of them not as an antiseptic academic, but rather as a daily user of them in his own professional and personal life. In our ever-changing society, with its disturbingly widening gap between the have and have not's, the needy and need not's, the power class and the disenfranchised, and the cared for and the careless, *Giving for Growth* inspires the reader to think about what the true blessings of success are and how they are to be used, and the mutual benefit that can ultimately be enjoyed by all of society's participants."

Bill Courtney, Author,
***Against the Grain,* Entrepreneur, and *Undefeated* Coach**

"In Jeremy, I saw a man who follows the words of John Wesley who long ago taught us: 'Do all the good you can, by all the means you can, in all the ways you can, in all the places you can, at all the times you can, to all the people you can….as long as ever you can.' In *Giving for Growth*, Jeremy charges us to do what is best, to be selfless, and to empty one's self so that others may live better lives."

Manny Diaz, former Mayor of Miami, Florida and Author,
***Miami Transformed: Rebuilding America One Neighborhood,*
*One City at a Time***

"*Giving for Growth* is a wonderful testimony that everything really comes down to people, and we must start with ourselves. I have had the joy of watching Jeremy live out the principles in the book and become a powerful agent of change in our community. Jeremy and this book will challenge and inspire you to find your passion, and they will give you practical steps to take to maximize your life, your business and the impact on your community."

Michael Drake, CEO
masterIT

"*Giving for Growth* highlights the many ways we can bring out the best in our teams, our communities and ourselves. In our increasingly polarized society, opportunities to connect with others and gain an appreciation and understanding for others' perspectives and experiences are more important than ever.

While some call it 'community leadership, volunteer service, or giving back,' it all brings value. Our companies, communities and children need us to step up, pay attention and get involved.

The need is real, the opportunities urgent and the rewards endless. The key for any organization or individual is finding something you want to do—and even better when you share that interest with and engage others. And keep *Giving for Growth* handy!"

Jenny Koltnow, Director, Communications & Community Relations, Customer Satisfaction AutoZone, Inc.

"*Giving for Growth* is a great book! Jeremy Park does an excellent job of capturing the positive ways in which giving back allows you grow personally and professionally while, at the same time, benefiting your community.

His thoughts on The Three Truths are not only very insightful but practical with a strategy that works. As a leader, I strive to stay ahead of the game; and so I enjoy reading about new approaches or innovations that might foster growth and development. This book definitely fosters growth and development, and it's not a theory! Jeremy Park writes from the strong foundation of facts and years of experience. I personally have seen Jeremy put these strategies into action within the community; and the proven success realized provides this book with a backdrop of credibility.

If you are a leader in any way, a CEO, pastor, teacher and, of course, a parent, this is a perfect read to help instill a message that will help you personally, but also help to continue the Greatness of our Country…We are the givers of the World."

Richard Montañez, Pepsi Sales North America, Creator of Flamin' Hot Cheetos

"The International Space Station (ISS) is an Orbital Outpost where astronauts from around the world come together to help advance our civilization. I had an opportunity to visit the ISS twice and on my first trip installed the European Space Agency's Columbus Laboratory, adding another large living component to the station, using the Canadian Space Agency's robotic arm, CanadaArm2. I thought that moment would be the crowning jewel of the mission but it's what happened next which changed me fundamentally. The commander of the ISS, Dr. Peggy Whitson invited our Space Shuttle crew over to the Russian Segment of the Space Station to have dinner. She said, 'You guys bring the rehydrated vegetables and we will supply the meat.' We gathered and dined together traveling around the planet at 17,500 miles per hour every 90 minutes, while breaking bread with people we used to fight against. I thought to myself if we can all get it together off-planet then there is no reason why we can't do that on Earth. My new Orbital Perspective made me want give back and share the view to let all know that our blue marble is really a small place where we can work together in peace and harmony. This mindset resonates so fundamentally with *Giving for Growth*."

**Dr. Leland Melvin, NASA Astronaut and S.T.E.A.M. Explorer
who flew on Space Shuttle Atlantis in 2008 and 2009**

"A compelling book with a distinctive and proven strategy to bring success to your personal life, your business and your community."

**Javier Peña, Talent & Leadership Developer,
Music Director of award-winning film, *For Once in My Life***

"In terms of talent recruitment, I can't think of any other transplant from the last 10 years that has had a more positive impact on our city than Jeremy Park. We are truly blessed he chooses to share his prodigious talents with our beloved community."

**Nancy Coffee, President and CEO,
New Memphis Institute**

DEDICATION

This book is dedicated to God, all my family and friends, and those who have been and continue to be integral parts of my life. It's lovingly dedicated, in particular, to my wife, Meredith, and our two boys, Cooper and Cayson. You three make me proud to be a husband and father; and I love you more than anything in life!

I further dedicate this book to those who are bravely serving our country to safeguard our lives and our freedoms; and to those who are searching for their own ways of giving back, helping others, and transforming this world for the betterment of all. I hope this book ignites a SPARK in your heart to think BIG, start small, and act NOW to start making your dreams reality!

• TABLE OF CONTENTS •

FOREWORD

For 55 years, every Wednesday morning at 6:00 AM sharp, my father, John Pitts, met with a group of his business friends at the Mark Twain Restaurant on Summer Avenue in Memphis, Tennessee. The purpose for their meeting was to work together in creating opportunities for young people who were less fortunate than them; but back then, that type of giving back was not en vogue. They saw things in a different light than most people, though. Their glass was half full...an optimist's perspective. In fact, the name of their organization was called the Optimist Club International; and my father helped found the Memphis Chapter.

What they understood was the importance of investing in their community. They visualized that one person could change the life of another person. But they also had the wherewithal to know that if their group and efforts were aligned with purpose, their impact would be magnified and many more lives could be changed in the process. Sometimes it took money, but what really created the change was their passion and mission to be the helping hands. They did not sit around the table and talk, nor pass their ideas to someone else to execute; they strategized and they, themselves acted to create the change and make a difference in the lives of others.

My father wasn't just a philanthropist; he was a keen businessman and visionary. He and Mr. Lipscomb II started Lipscomb & Pitts Insurance in 1954 with just one employee. It's astonishing to see where we are more than 60 years later. Since Mat Lipscomb III and I purchased the business from our fathers in 1992, we have grown the business to nearly 150 employees, representing over 250 insurance carriers. Today, we are the largest privately-held brokerage firm in the Mid-South and among the top 100 in our nation. We are recognized as an industry top workplace by *Insurance Journal*, Key Risk, IIABA, and *Insurance Business*. We are also regularly recognized by several local publications like The Memphis Business Journal and The Commercial Appeal, and nationally by *Forbes* Magazine for reasons relating to leadership, company culture, and business success.

In my years running Lipscomb & Pitts Insurance and being very involved in the community from nonprofits to politics, I have seen the landscape of business change. Corporate philanthropy is becoming a priority. In fact, as you will learn in this book, social impact and purpose is now mandatory. Like Rich Karlgaard states in his book, *The Soft Edge*, there is so much more to the success of a company than the balance sheet, profit and loss statements, and even charitable giving. It's the culture and how a company provides ways for employees to engage in the community. Younger generations, like the Millennials, have an ingrained desire and drive to volunteer and make an impact; but many don't know how or where to start. It's up to business and community leaders to guide our employees, to encourage them, and most importantly, to lead by example.

Most people entering the workforce today are looking for more than a job, more than a career; they want fulfillment. They're asking, "Does my work have meaning beyond my paycheck; do I have the ability to develop meaningful relationships within my hometown to help people in need?"

Eight years ago, I met a young radio marketing and advertising salesman who had just moved to town from Los Angeles, California. Within the first minutes of meeting Jeremy Park, it was evident he had a heart for service. More and more, I noticed him around the community as a collaborator, bringing people together through business and community efforts. Not long after that first meeting, I invited him to my office; but it was not to discuss advertising.

Together, Jeremy and I laid out a vision and plan for where we could take a business networking organization I had helped establish in Memphis in 2005, known back then as the Lipscomb Pitts Breakfast Club. After a series of events leading to Lipscomb & Pitts Insurance becoming the sole owner of the Lipscomb Pitts Breakfast Club, we needed someone to bring this new vision and plan to life; and that person was Jeremy Park.

Person to person, company to company, we have been focused on changing the way people think about improving our community. It started with subtle changes that have now grown into a larger cause, opening the floodgates so our whole community can participate. Now, we are known as cityCURRENT (we rebranded the organization in 2016 and set it up as a separate LLC) and we host over 150 events a year, have a weekly newspaper column, radio show, TV show, book, televised awards show, and now this second book. And yet, because our purpose remains grounded in helping people, we know the best is still to come!

Thinking and acting philanthropically not only changes our hearts, it ultimately changes our neighborhoods, cities, states, and nation; and it all starts with leadership. This book explains the why's and how's of corporate involvement....why you should do it, but most importantly, how you can do it in a way that becomes part of your culture and a way of thinking for your employees, even when they leave the office. As the momentum of their passion increases, all things become possible because of one person deciding that someone or some organization needed help; and now many others begin to follow. With persistence, you will reach a tipping point where that momentum will sweep you away, but in a way that benefits everyone in the community.

My father used to say "Don't stop water running down a hill." The ever increasing number of companies and people who are giving back is creating a tidal wave of positive energy and actions. If we channel that water to become accessible to everyone we can change the world! So, use this book as your field guide to chart your own course, access the water, and channel it to make a difference in your community and the lives of others. Your adventure will be unforgettable, but best of all, your impact will be monumental!

PRELUDE

I've dedicated most of my life to helping others and giving back to my community. This has been immensely rewarding; and it's enabled me to realize all my childhood dreams. I've been fortunate, too, to have worked with numerous business and entertainment icons, each of whom have helped shape my expectations of and perspectives on how corporations can be catalysts for good in their community.

As a youth, I lived most of my years in Weatherford, Texas. In retrospect, something that always stood out was that my parents had an open door policy toward people in our community. At any hour of the day or night, they would warmly welcome into our home families and individuals who were facing challenges and needed help or support. My brother, Jeff, and I experienced firsthand, in these moments, the importance of helping others. We saw that my parents became trusted advisors and friends to many people in Weatherford; and, consequently, the more people they helped, the more doors of opportunity seemed to be opened for our family. We also noticed that most times the issues people faced and things they needed help with were not related to my father's job in the insurance industry or my mother's professional experience; rather, they sought "personal" advice and empathy. Once again, though, there was a correlation where the more my parents helped "personally," the more successful they became "professionally."

My parents, of course, made many sacrifices to allow my brother and me to follow our dreams, especially when it came to tennis and Boy Scouts. As a youth and young adult, I was privileged to be able to play competitive tennis and to travel throughout our nation and other countries around the world for tournaments.

When Jeff and I wanted to join the Boy Scout program, my parents readily volunteered and served as den, pack, and troop leaders so we could learn the values of the Scout Law and what it truly means to be "trustworthy, loyal, helpful, friendly, courteous, kind, obedient, cheerful, thrifty, brave, clean, and reverent." I still have fond memories of hiking and camping at Philmont Scout Ranch in Cimarron, New Mexico, and enjoying activities like archery, swimming, and sailing at summer camp.

Although I ultimately chose competitive tennis over Boy Scouts, I give much credit to the Boy Scout program for equipping me with a mindset of service and the skills to lead by example. I'm proud that my brother, Jeff, earned the rank of Eagle Scout and that my parents continue to volunteer their time to the Scout program, long after their children have left home. My father, in particular, has helped thousands of young men develop their character and leadership potential; and our nation is much better for it! And, yes, my parents still maintain that open door policy!

While in college (first at Baylor University and then at the University of North Texas), I was actively involved in a host of organizations that championed volunteerism. I did well balancing these activities with tennis and the priority of my academics; but since I was also pursuing my childhood dreams of playing music in a band and acting in movies and commercials, I needed to find time in an already hectic schedule to write songs and practice my craft. It was in college that I developed the basis for my ideology of "Three Daily Steps" – doing three things each day that would move me forward and closer to fulfilling my dreams. This meant that I wouldn't go to sleep until three things, such as practicing a monologue, completing a song chorus, or meeting someone new had been accomplished. This mindset of small, daily steps – consistent, persistent progression – has stayed with me to this day. I still don't go to sleep until three things have been done to move our organization or our community forward.

After graduating from the University of North Texas with a degree in Marketing, I took on a job as Director of Marketing for a television production company based in Valencia, California. During my college days, I had made a favorable impression on someone in Texas who knew the owner of this production company and had opened the door for this first step in my career. The person I had impressed was Sharon Campbell, my acting coach, who saw me at her studio just about every day and also saw me raising my hand to help market programs and performances, clean the school, and set up for showcases. I was willing to do anything that needed to be done to help her studio succeed. Sharon told the owner of the production company that "If this young man can sell out a show with local, unknown actors, he can surely market your shows with well-known talent." So, the day after graduation, I was headed to California!

Two years after I started working at the television production company, the business took on a project in Florida and decided to relocate. I opted to remain in Los Angeles to pursue my dreams of music and acting; but that decision presented me with new challenges. I was now jobless and had very few connections. Instead of engaging in my community, I had completely immersed myself in my work and career. In a city of ten million people, I knew only a handful. Providence was on my side, though! I inadvertently showed up one morning at the wrong tennis courts, where I thought a drop-in match would be taking place. I never found the intended match, but was fortunate to meet a charismatic tennis player with a huge heart, "Big Wave" Dave Lanz. He instantly welcomed me into his life – and family – and made it his mission to introduce me to everyone he knew around town.

Through Dave's connections and that of one of my former tennis coaches, I soon received a call from Trevor Sands, the Director of Tennis at Beverly Hills Country Club. He simply said, "If you want to teach tennis, we'd love to have you join our team." Talk about a miracle and a dream job for someone who'd grown up playing competitive tennis! It was further proof that a distinct correlation existed between relationships with people and opportunities in life. Dave Lanz and my former tennis coach had reached out to others, on my behalf, to open a door that ultimately allowed me to fulfill my dreams and meet people who would become more than friends; they became family.

As a tennis professional at Beverly Hills Country Club, I took great pride in my work conducting private lessons and group clinics, organizing adult and junior competitive teams, and hosting tournaments and summer camps. I volunteered to help wherever I could because I knew that doing even the smallest things, such as picking up litter on the courts, would somehow pay off in the long run. Ironically, it was when I was cleaning the courts late one afternoon after a tennis tournament that Trevor Sands walked by and commented that he appreciated my work ethic, positive attitude, and leadership potential. He then invited me to serve as the Head Tennis Professional at Beverly Hills Country Club.

Being named Head Tennis Pro was a blessing because it gave me the opportunity to step back and run the club's programs with freedom and flexibility. I was able to take time off to do short tours with my band or to spend a few days acting in movies. My elevated position at the club also afforded me the distinct privilege of working with entertainment icon, Merv Griffin, and running his celebrity tennis tournaments, which were held at the Beverly Hills Country Club and featured celebrity players like Matthew Perry and Dr. Phil. Being the Head Pro had other awesome perks, too. I played tennis with Sir Ridley Scott (the English film director and producer of *Alien* fame, as well as *Gladiator*, and *Black Hawk Down*) and gave private tennis lessons to Paula and Paul Reiser at their home court in the Hollywood Hills. Paul Reiser is the comedian, actor, writer, and television personality most widely known for his role in the TV sitcom, *Mad About You*. Getting to know this couple and their family was an immense pleasure.

The five years I worked at the Beverly Hills Country Club was a period of great personal growth for me and a magical time when all my childhood dreams had come true. I played tennis among the stars. I performed music, which I had written, on famous stages, in front of thousands of people who actually sang the songs back even louder than we were playing them. I acted in movies and in national television commercials. I made friends who shared in my journey and became like brothers and sisters to me in the process. What I had achieved, though, had been dependent on others believing in me and giving me opportunities to succeed.

In retrospect, I wasn't that great an actor. I didn't have the greatest talent when it came to playing guitar, singing, and writing songs; but I DID work hard, was dependable, and always showed up on time, ready to perform. My band and I understood marketing.

We knew that our job was to put on a show that entertained and engaged the audience. People in power trusted that my band and I would do whatever it took to sell out shows and make each song and performance memorable. It also didn't hurt that we had created a vast network of friends, who supported one another and helped us promote our shows!

One concert in particular holds a bittersweet memory for me. Our group opened for a rock band that I had idolized as a youth. The concert was an exhilarating experience but also a deflating, defining moment, as I realized that this was not the future I wanted for me and the family I hoped to have at some point. That band admittedly was only playing the show to make ends meet; and the stories they were sharing were of the "good old days," not about the future. This, for me, signaled a change in the course of my life.

Our band, which had already given me more than what I ever thought was possible, was beginning to drift apart. The night we played our last show at a KROQ (Los Angeles, California Alternative Rock radio station) event at Universal City Walk, we were given an encore. After we walked off stage, we officially called it quits.

Shortly after our band broke up, my tennis career came to a screeching halt, as well. I was playing in a doubles tournament with one of my best friends, Anthony Cava. We were tied with our opponents one set apiece and were in position to win the third set and match as I stepped up to the baseline to serve. I tossed up the ball, swung to hit a kick-serve, and my shoulder completely gave out. It hurt so bad that I couldn't continue the match and so we had to default. My shoulder has never been the same since.

Needless to say, reality sometimes hits hard. The reality for me was that my time with tennis, music, and acting had all come to an end. It was tough looking at myself in the mirror knowing that all the time invested and everything I had sacrificed and worked so hard to achieve would only be memories. I realized then that I needed to change course and return to the corporate world. So, I did exactly what I'm now encouraging you to do – I started volunteering. Since my strength was my talent for marketing, I offered to help with marketing projects and committees. This strategically placed me with business leaders who could open new doors for me along the career path I was seeking. It didn't take long for me to get back into media and land a job with a local sports radio station. This employment soon led to an even more exclusive opportunity – working with a part of Dick Clark's legacy, United Stations Radio Networks, which specializes in nationally syndicated radio programs.

It was around that time when life threw me a "beautiful" curve ball! One of my grade school friends, Molly Harris, was working on her doctorate degree at Mississippi State University. Molly and I were talking on the phone one day when she jokingly passed her phone to one of her friends and fellow students, Meredith. My relationship with Meredith started with fun teasing and her trying to convince me to fly into Memphis, Tennessee to visit Starkville, Mississippi. After a few weeks of long-distance calls, I saw a picture of Meredith; and then, I immediately was flying to meet her! The rest is history. Meredith and I are now happily married and have two wonderful boys (and a dog and pond filled with fish). I couldn't be happier!

An important decision Meredith and I had to make was regarding where we wanted to call home and raise a family. Meredith's close-knit family lives in Corinth, Mississippi; so we explored all the larger city options within a reasonable distance of Corinth. Ultimately, we decided that the Memphis area was the best fit for us. Since neither of us really knew anyone in Memphis, we both began putting out feelers. Meredith eventually took a teaching job with DeSoto County Schools in Southaven, Mississippi. I utilized one of my radio connections through United Stations Radio Networks and landed a job doing local radio sales and promotions for Clear Channel Radio, now known as iHeartMedia, in Memphis.

Once again, I was living and working in a city where I knew virtually no one. And again, I did precisely what I am recommending in this book. I took that easy, first step. I started volunteering and getting engaged with nonprofits. I asked business owners and executives to sit down with me over coffee almost every day so I could learn more about their businesses and offer them whatever help or resource I could. Being a newcomer, I couldn't provide connections; but I could provide a fresh perspective and share ideas that I had seen work well in cities like Los Angeles, New York, and the Dallas-Fort Worth Metroplex.

This is how I met Johnny Pitts, Chief Manager of Lipscomb & Pitts Insurance. As luck would have it, we moved to the Memphis area in 2007, which was around the time Lipscomb & Pitts Insurance bought out the franchise rights for an organization known at the time as the Lipscomb Pitts Breakfast Club, a business-networking group that hosted national guest speakers at a Signature Breakfast Series with the goal of "Developing business relationships. Period." In 2005, Johnny had been approached by a franchisee of Breakfast Club of America to start a chapter in Memphis. Lipscomb & Pitts Insurance stepped up as title sponsor to establish the Lipscomb Pitts Breakfast Club. In 2007, Breakfast Club of America started to dissolve, allowing franchisees across the nation to purchase their territory rights and take full ownership of their organizations. Johnny saw this as the perfect opportunity to buy out the Mid-South franchise rights from corporate and also the franchisee, in order to bring the Lipscomb Pitts Breakfast Club in house as a division of Lipscomb & Pitts Insurance.

At the same time, I was getting to know Amy Bingham. Amy served as the Director of Communications at Lipscomb & Pitts Insurance during the aforementioned transition of the Breakfast Club ownership. She and Johnny had invited me to attend some of the Signature Breakfast Series events in order to get my thoughts for improving it; and we were already starting to explore ideas to expand outside of the Signature Breakfast Series in order to add more value, like with moderated executive lunches. My viewpoint was that if the organization was focused solely on business networking with no higher purpose, it was only a matter of time before it ran the risk of becoming irrelevant. To me, relevance can only be maintained through PURPOSE, one that is directly tied to benefiting people, especially those within a given community.

My relationship with Johnny Pitts and Amy Bingham proved the pivotal point for the amazing career I enjoy today. When Amy's husband, Russell Bingham, received an opportunity to take the next step in his career in a new city, Amy and Johnny sat down to talk about who might be able to step in and lead the organization with her departure. That's when Johnny called and asked if I would consider writing the business and marketing plan for the Lipscomb Pitts Breakfast Club and then step in as the Director. The caveat, though, was that there was no real money to pay me to lead the organization since Lipscomb & Pitts Insurance had just purchased the rights and there were only a handful of businesses participating and less than 20 events being hosted each year. So, the compromise was that I could step into Amy's vacated position and oversee the communications efforts for Lipscomb & Pitts Insurance and then, on the side, see where I could take this small networking organization called the Lipscomb Pitts Breakfast Club.

Almost a decade later, I'm now the Vice President of Communications and a Member of the LLC for Lipscomb & Pitts Insurance. Instead of being a "one man show," there's a full team in place handling all of the marketing, communications, and charitable efforts for the largest independent insurance agency in the Mid-South and one of the largest independent agencies in the nation.

Today, most people know me, though, for my role as President of cityCURRENT, which is a privately-funded catalyst focused on philanthropy, free community events and positive-oriented media; all with the mission of being "a force for good." cityCURRENT is the evolution of the Lipscomb Pitts Breakfast Club, which we rebranded in 2016 and set up as a separate entity, in order to become even more strategically aimed at making as much of a difference as possible. As President, I direct a partnership of more than 80 businesses, which includes some of the world's largest employers, such as FedEx, AutoZone, ServiceMaster, and Smith & Nephew. These corporate partners combine forces and funds to give back charitably and to underwrite and host an array of media and over 150 events each year that enrich and impact our community. For perspective, in 2014, we hosted 192 events; and in 2015, we hosted 184 events! Such phenomenal teamwork has transformed what was once a small, simple business-networking group into a powerhouse that is now recognized around the world as an innovator in corporate philanthropy, social entrepreneurialism, and collective impact.

cityCurrent has five fundamental tenets:
1) Strategic Corporate Philanthropy – Bringing businesses together to align resources and efforts to make a collective impact in the

community; 2) Strategic Collaboration – Bringing professionals and leaders from all facets of our city – business, nonprofit, education, government, and faith – together to foster collaboration; 3) FREE Community Events – Making it easy for all citizens to become more engaged by offering, at no charge to attendees, public events that enrich and give back to others; 4) Turnkey Volunteerism – Providing turnkey opportunities for individuals of all ages, along with companies and their employees, to become more engaged in the community; 5) Positive Media – Providing a pipeline for uplifting stories to be shared and media outlets to spread good news, inspiration, and opportunities for engagement in the community.

So, our cityCURRENT team works tirelessly to host seminars and workshops, bring in national guest speakers with our Signature Breakfast and Signature Speaker Series, and host weekly executive lunches and other events that provide valuable content and foster collaboration among business, education, government, faith, and nonprofit leaders. Our corporate partners fully underwrite these events, so no admittance fee is ever charged to attendees.

We also give financially and provide turnkey opportunities for companies and individuals to become more engaged in the community; and we leverage our resources to make an impact through volunteer days, action projects, nonprofit tours, fundraising, and more. Examples of these opportunities include tutoring after school, mentoring, removing graffiti from buildings and bridges, washing the feet of almost 3,000 kids and providing them with new socks and shoes, assisting in the organization of over 12,000 volunteers to beautify the city during a three-day work session and then helping to remove over 90,000 pounds of trash at McKellar Lake, spearheading a Fallen Officer Memorial, creating and promoting the Power of the Dollar Campaign ("buy local"), launching a civic pride effort called "Memphis Rocks," and hosting a Film Festival screening and telethon. We're heavily focused on sharing positive news, showcasing those leading by example, and encouraging engagement. At this point, you've probably surmised that our media plays an important role in ensuring the success of these endeavors, too!

Each Sunday you can read my "Giving Back" column in The Commercial Appeal. The column, launched in 2010, spotlights the efforts of local nonprofits and offers creative ways for citizens to weave giving back into their everyday life and business routine. The column is also sometimes featured in their Weeklies, which are distributed, at no charge, to households across the Mid-South. The hundreds of "Giving Back" columns I've written over the past five years served as the basis for my first book, *Giving Back with Purpose: Fueling Growth through Community Involvement*, and also provided the foundation for this book.

Main Street Books published and released *Giving Back with Purpose* in 2013. The book publicizes the efforts of organizations and individuals in the Mid-South who are giving back; and it provides a blueprint for helping the readers construct their own legacy of making a difference. Because all the proceeds benefit youth literacy programs in the Mid-South, the book about giving back to others actually gives back to others! Among the groups that have received funding as a result of *Giving Back with Purpose* are Binghampton Christian Academy, Shelby County Books from Birth, and the Community Foundation of Northwest Mississippi's "Excel by 5" program. Like this book, *Giving Back with Purpose* is available online and through select retailers; so with the continued support of readers like YOU, we can continue giving back to our local, youth-serving literacy programs.

Another media format that we utilize for sharing and promoting the good and for expanding the ideology of giving back is radio with our cityCURRENT radio show, which first launched in 2011. Our show airs each Sunday, from 7 AM to 8 AM, across all four Cumulus Media Memphis' radio stations, which have over 750,000 listeners weekly and include 98.1 THE MAX, 98.9 THE VIBE, KIX 106, and 103.5 WRBO. If you live outside the Mid-South, you can stream the show online or listen via their station apps. Our broadcasts focus on positive influences in our area and feature various business and community leaders who discuss important efforts, projects, news, and trends. To listen to past shows and archived interviews, visit the Media Center section of our website, cityCURRENT.com. The Cumulus Media Memphis team, along with each of our cityCURRENT partners, shares our dedication to celebrate and raise awareness of the GOOD things taking place in our community every day.

Knowing the power of television, in 2013 we teamed with our cityCURRENT partner and local PBS affiliate, WKNO-TV, to launch and produce a television show, The SPARK. This 30-minute program airs the third Friday of each month at 7:30 PM on WKNO/Channel 10. We concentrate on positive happenings in the Mid-South and feature organizations and individuals who are leading by example to ignite change for good. We also focus on volunteerism and how viewers can help make a difference. It's important to note that we're not only working to underwrite this positive-oriented programming, but we're also fully involved in the production of each episode, from booking the guests to interacting on camera as host. This level of engagement is important because it helps us personalize the message and ensure success.

In 2014, we expanded The SPARK to include an annual televised awards show, The SPARK Awards. This special telecast celebrates and honors organizations and individuals who exemplify the power of giving back through their efforts to make a positive impact in the Mid-South. There are 13 different categories of awards covering corporations, nonprofits, schools, education leaders, teachers, youth, college students, and adult volunteers. There's even a SPARK Legacy Award to celebrate an individual's lifetime of philanthropic leadership. To make it truly community-driven, the public nominates all of the candidates; and then special selection committees from the Midtown Memphis Rotary Club ultimately choose the honorees. The show is produced in partnership between cityCURRENT and WKNO-TV. It's been a pleasure working with the production teams to bring both The SPARK and The SPARK Awards to life; and it's been rewarding to have numerous businesses show their support through sponsorship and to have many organizations align as promotional partners, too.

Overall, cityCURRENT interacts with more than 50,000 leaders across the Mid-South on a weekly basis. We've proven that media, like a newspaper column, radio show, and television series, focused on sharing good news and ways citizens can become positively engaged in their communities can be a BIG success! Hopefully, our success will encourage more media outlets nationwide to produce similar shows that accentuate the positives in our country and will inspire other organizations and individuals to take charge in creating these types of opportunities for their hometowns.

So, persistent focus on community service and giving back has opened wide, countless doors of rewarding opportunities for me personally and professionally. The dream I'm striving to fulfill now is to make life better for people in my community and to make Memphis a place my two boys are proud to call home. My goal is to be a SPARK who ignites in others the passion for giving back so that more citizens are inspired to become actively engaged in creating a better society. My involvement in cityCURRENT has shown me that having purpose as an organization and as an individual is critical to success and sustainability. The fun now is that I can share with you some of the lessons we've learned and the strategies and tactics that we use daily to promote a mindset of Giving for Growth. Let's start with The Three Truths.

GIVING for GROWTH

Chapter One

THE THREE TRUTHS

We live in a fast-paced, hyper-connected world. Professionals and executives are under constant siege from ambitious goals and tight timelines. We have access to endless data that's designed to help us make better decisions, yet often lead us to data overload and paralysis by analysis. We sit in strategic planning meetings most of the day, use lots of bullet points, and have become laser focused on the Return On Investment (ROI) for our efforts. This has conditioned us to get straight to the point. So, I'm going to start by addressing the most important thing you should take away from this book. Even if you read no further than The Three Truths, you will have gleaned the fundamental principles for achieving more meaningful success in both business and life.

I can write this with utmost confidence because once I myself discovered these Three Truths and how they were interconnected, I became more purposeful in my day-to-day actions; and this transformed my life! My hope is that the lessons, strategies, and tactics shared in this book will transform your life, too, as you adopt the tenets and mindset of Giving for Growth. Infusing purpose into the things you're already doing, so that your activities benefit others, can be fun and easier than you think. Being strategic with your approach to giving back allows you to maximize the inherent rewards and impact you can make with your efforts while creating a tangible ROI for your career and life. The best part about these Three Truths is that everybody involved wins! The more you help others and invest in your community, the more good will come your way. The more good befalls you, the more you will be able to help others and your community. This kind of return becomes immeasurable!

Let's get started, then, by looking at The Three Truths that serve as the foundation for Giving for Growth.

TRUTH 1: PEOPLE PHYSICALLY SOLVE PROBLEMS

While money is a powerful resource, it does not, on its own, solve a single problem. If you put a dollar bill on the table, it cannot walk, talk, or interact. PEOPLE are the true catalysts for solving problems. There is no substitute for this truth.

Corporately, the charge for business owners, executives and managers is to apply this truth to their organizations and to lead by example. Leaders must make it easy for their employees, who can become an army of do-gooders and problem solvers, to volunteer their time, talents, and treasures to make a difference in the community. When leaders create a culture of giving back within their organization, the ensuing benefits can be substantial. As employees start investing in their community and rolling up their sleeves to make a difference, the transformation affected by such benevolent behavior enriches the lives of the employees and their families, creates a bond and feeling of loyalty and pride between business and community, and improves the overall well-being of the community itself – all of which is mutually beneficial to the organization.

Anyone who wants to see change, however, must be willing to BE the change. It starts with the individual. The level of impact is not what's important, especially at the beginning; it's the willingness to get involved. In order for us to live in a vibrant community, each of us must get physically involved in giving back. This requires a personal commitment to showing up, being engaged, and understanding that we're all connected in a broader sense of "community."

TRUTH 2: PEOPLE PROVIDE OPPORTUNITIES FOR PEOPLE

Just as PEOPLE physically solve problems, it's also true that PEOPLE provide opportunities for PEOPLE. No one creates success on his or her own. Each of us is the product of the people we surround ourselves with and the communities in which we live. You might work for a great organization and make a tremendous impact through your business; however, someone originally believed in you and provided you the opportunity to succeed. So, the underlying truth is that having opportunities to grow comes down to PEOPLE. The more you as an individual are able to interact with others, build trust and credibility, and showcase your unique talents and expertise, the more likely doors of opportunity will be opened for you. This holds true both on a professional and personal level. The more dedicated you become to the precept of Giving for Growth, the more probable you are to connect with the people around you, thereby broadening your network of personal relationships.

We'll expand on this in future chapters, but decide today to think and act with a positive attitude. Build up others around you. Encourage them to grow along with you. This kind of attitude is inspiring and contagious, drawing people in like a magnet; and it can affect surprising, favorable outcomes! The more you surround yourself with people who have a similar mindset and who fully commit themselves to community service, the more opportunities for growth and success these combined efforts will generate for everyone — a win-win-win outcome.

TRUTH 3: GIVING BACK WILL GET YOU AHEAD

Giving back through community engagement is always the right thing to do; however, your ROI for this engagement can be exponential – the more you give, the more you'll receive. Giving back moves you forward. It super charges your life and business and propels you further down the road to success than you could imagine. GIVING allows you to GROW!

Giving for Growth leverages the first two truths. I steadfastly believe that the best way to broaden your personal relationships and to expand your sphere of positive influence is by GIVING BACK. Volunteering fosters understanding of and empathy for others. It provides an underpinning for building bonds of trust between you and the people with whom you are working; it creates a sense of being part of a bigger cause than yourself;

and it empowers you to become a more productive part of your organization and community.

While the philanthropic value and personal growth benefits of giving back are becoming more appreciated by organizations today, another, purely practical, reason exists for the growing popularity of corporate volunteerism. Consumers are increasingly making purchases based on corporate engagement. In the modern marketplace, people are paying attention to the purpose or storyline behind products and services. Since people buy goods and services from people and organizations based on trust, businesses are ultimately tasked with building and maintaining customers' trust. Successful businesses understand this; and servant leaders wisely recognize that trust demands a selfless attitude and a commitment to sustaining the integrity of one's word and actions. Volunteerism serves as an ideal avenue for nurturing these desirable qualities in people. When employees accept and honor a commitment to physically get engaged in their community so that its citizens' lives are enriched, then those citizens who have been positively impacted often return the favor by supporting the organization.

The bottom line is this: organizations that seek to hire servant leaders who encourage community engagement and employees who commit to volunteerism are among the most successful and fastest growing businesses in the new marketplace. Do you aspire to create a similar outlook for your business?

MAKE THE MAGIC HAPPEN

People solve problems; and people provide opportunities for people. Once you understand that your physical engagement is essential for improving the lives of others and subsequently that engagement will make your own personal and professional life more rewarding – that's when the magic can happen.

Volunteerism provides an ideal conduit for honing your problem-solving skills and developing important bonds of trust that are mutually beneficial to you and those with whom you work. It allows you to meet new people and build enduring relationships with people who can open doors of opportunity for your future success.

That's how giving back can get you ahead! The next step is to develop a strategy so you can be deliberate in your actions and begin creating a legacy of helping others while growing personally and professionally.

Before I address strategy and share examples and tactics, however, let me show why all of this should matter to you and your organization. I think you'll find the following trends in corporate philanthropy quite interesting.

THOUGHTS & ACTION STEPS

Chapter Two

TRENDS IN CORPORATE PHILANTHROPY

A few years ago, I had the chance to interview my friend, Richard Smith, who is Managing Director of Life Sciences for FedEx Express and the son of FedEx Founder, Chairman, President, and CEO, Fred Smith. I asked him if there were important lessons that he learned from his father that he could pass along as advice to others. One of Richard's answers was an adaptation of the famous military adage, known as the "7 Ps" – "Proper Planning and Preparation Prevents Piss Poor Performance." This adage has myriad variations now with the "5 Ps" and Fred Smith's personal "6 Ps;" but just like the famous Boy Scout Motto, "Be Prepared," proper preparation is an indispensable key to success in life and business.

For this reason, it's important to understand the trends taking place in corporate philanthropy and cause marketing. It'll help you construct the proper framework for leveraging these trends to make sound decisions for today and for the future. You'll find these trends can be applied to you as an individual and to your organization, as well.

SOCIAL IMPACT AND PURPOSE IS NOW MANDATORY

In the past, corporate philanthropy primarily entailed writing a check. Today, however, business leaders and consumers alike have become much more discerning with heightened expectations for strategic reinvestment, physical engagement, and community impact. This means businesses must be proactive by reaching out, building partnerships with nonprofits, and leading charitable efforts, rather than being reactive and waiting for an organization to ask for support. It also means corporations must explore ways they can leverage ALL available resources for the greater good. This includes financial capital, human resources, and physical assets like buildings, conference centers, and equipment – all of which can be valuable to organizations serving the community. So, corporate philanthropy today is much more proactive and strategic, combining both financial funding and physical engagement to make a quantifiable impact in the community.

The significance of this supports the first of The Three Truths – understanding that money is a desired resource, but that people are needed to physically solve problems. Due in part to our country's financial and economic crisis, which began in December 2007, consumers have realized the need for business leaders to take a far more encompassing approach in thinking long term and addressing larger social issues that government alone cannot solve, such as health and wellness, education, and the environment. Corporate philanthropy has made many national headlines; but the bottom line is that consumers are now looking at Corporate America to be a part of the solution for our local and national problems. In fact, I'll take it a step further and say consumers now fully expect businesses to help create sustainable solutions; and they want to see proof of it, i.e. at volunteer events and on social media.

Our cityCURRENT hosts annual Samaritan's Feet Shoe Distributions, which provide the perfect example of the importance of being an active, visible participant in charitable efforts. Hundreds of adult volunteers come out to these events to wash the feet of Memphis youth and provide them with new socks and shoes. These volunteers are business and community leaders, college students, athletes, active military personnel, and retired individuals; so it's a wonderful cross-section of our city. At one of the events, a Human Resources Manager from a very large company headquartered here in Memphis was commenting on how much he loved attending the events because they were filled with compassion and joy. He then added, "And I love seeing who else is out here serving with us because these are the types of people we want to hire and do business with." What a powerful testimonial to the importance of being directly involved and being seen actively giving back to our community.

This type of open engagement in the community creates not just goodwill; it holds significant financial implications, as well. With increasing frequency, today's consumers are deciding where to purchase goods and services based on social impact. Tom Shadyac, the Hollywood Producer and Director of such mega hits as *Bruce Almighty, Ace Ventura: Pet Detective, Liar Liar, Nutty Professor*, and *Patch Adams* says it simply comes down to "love." He notes:

"Wal-Mart will become All-Mart and Starbucks will become Ourbucks because if they aren't giving back, another business will; and by the natural heartstring pull, we will choose to do business with the one focused on love. Every single one of us will shop at All-Mart or Ourbucks because it shares its resources with the community. It's not going to create a super wealthy class, it's going to create wealth by giving back to the community. All-Mart and Ourbucks are places we'll shop because we'll know our dollars are staying to educate kids. That doesn't mean the CEO of All-Mart and Ourbucks aren't going to do incredibly well. The CEOs will get everything they need to rock their lives. We want diversity in life and business; but the All-Mart and Ourbucks CEOs will go the grave with a 9.9 on the happiness scale because they shared their love."

Sharing love and having a purpose that focuses on others is powerful! If you and your company are not helping others, then, at some point, another company – perhaps one of your competitors – WILL; and consumers will follow their hearts and choose to do business with the entity exhibiting a higher purpose, the one sharing and showing "love."

My wife and I are examples of consumers who make purchasing decisions based on social impact. Before making a purchase, we search online to find places that have a focus on giving back and supporting charitable efforts. We purposefully buy certain products, like shampoo, food, and articles of clothing because that purchase will benefit a nonprofit. We'll eat at certain restaurants on nights where a percentage of the meal's cost or proceeds are donated; and we'll intentionally select gifts that have a unique storyline and higher purpose.

In light of this trend, business leaders would be prudent to take to heart a comment made by Brent Bushnell, a lifelong engineer and entrepreneur who is currently the CEO of Two Bit Circus, Inc. His dictum appeared in Evan Kirkpatrick's *Forbes* column entitled "3 Key Elements of Capitalist Philanthropy." What was Bushnell's statement?

"Companies without social impact culture will soon be obsolete."

Even more food for thought is presented to us by this quote from *Forbes* Publisher, Rich Karlgaard's recent book, *The Soft Edge*: "For the first time in history, impressions of openness, sincerity and authenticity are more important to corporate reputation in the United States than the quality of products and services." Karlgaard's observation is germane to this chapter's topic because it ascribes the human qualities of "openness, sincerity and authenticity" to businesses. No longer impersonal entities narrowly focused on producing quality goods and services, companies have "evolved" and are now viewed as citizens within a community. Consequently, they will be held to similar expectations that we have for each other, as humans, as citizens, as neighbors. It is expedient, then, that companies welcome this new role in society and embrace the spirit of giving back.

Changing attitudes about business-community relations are not limited to consumers. Today's job-seekers, especially those of the Millennial generation, are now choosing where they want to work based on a company's social engagement and impact. Part of their expectation is having the flexibility to use company time for their volunteer service rather than to sacrifice precious time for family and friends during the weekend or after work. If your business hasn't yet encountered such a request, be forewarned. It's coming!

We'll explore tactics for corporations in a later chapter, but this expectation of flexibility from employees necessitates changes, especially if you hope to compete for top talent. As a result, businesses are now offering things like modified work schedules, where employees can volunteer in the morning and arrive at work later or they can leave work early and volunteer for the last hour of the workday. It also entails hosting things, like food, clothing, and toy drives at the office, raising money with "Casual Days," and scheduling a variety of nonprofit tours, action projects, and other activities that make a difference. To attract and retain the best talent, progressive business leaders understand they must exemplify and encourage physical engagement and social impact. The good news is studies show that when companies offer these types of programs and opportunities, employee morale and productivity increase. That's a tangible benefit for the business!

Looking at the traditional marketing mix model, you'll always see the four Ps, representing Product, Price, Place, and Promotion. The model has been expanded to include People, Process, and Position; but the next extension will include "Purpose" because purpose is no longer just the icing on the cake. Purpose has become one of the fundamental ingredients for success. Consequently, the key to growth is in determining your purpose. Give your company, product, service, and even yourself a competitive edge by defining your purpose and then setting out to find ways you can breathe life into that purpose and sustain its growth so you, your business, and your community collectively benefit.

FOCUSING ON MISSION AND SKILLSET ALIGNMENT

Focus is fundamental to success in sports, business, and life. It's a facilitator for all learning, reasoning, problem solving, and decision-making. Focus is what allows us to be creative and productive; it helps us avoid distractions and stay attentive to the task at hand. Focus is also becoming one of the important trends in corporate philanthropy.

To achieve corporate success, business leaders understand they must strategically make the most effective, efficient use of their limited resources and invest in areas with the highest probability of return. These leaders are making similar decisions regarding their charitable efforts. They are selecting nonprofits based on mission alignment and narrowing their scope to support a smaller number of organizations in a more meaningful way.

Instead of a business spreading its financial contributions

thinly over hundreds of nonprofits, that same business now is working strategically with fewer organizations to make a more significant impact. Companies of all sizes are hand-picking areas of concentration, like education, disaster response, safety, cultural arts, and environmental sustainability. Then, they are closely aligning themselves with those select nonprofits in order to achieve the greatest ROI. This trend stems from many different factors; but one of the most important is that business leaders are driven by results. They desire and are accustomed to seeing tangible returns on their investments, including financial, human, and physical assets. In order to see these types of returns in a larger social context, though, larger investments must be made; so business leaders are adopting a more focused approach to achieve better results.

Business leaders are also going a step further by strategically aligning the skillsets of their employees with the needs of nonprofits. A company in Memphis that specializes in logistics, for example, is working with an organization that ships medical supplies around the world, offering their technical and operational expertise for strategic planning with the board and training for the nonprofit's team. The company also is helping by supplying the software and program applications for tracking, and then providing volunteers to prepare the boxes for shipment. This alignment of skillsets and expertise produces synergistic results where the level of impact is much greater.

IT'S EVEN MORE THAN TIME AND MONEY

Businesses have a wealth of assets they can use to make a difference in their communities. They have financial resources to make contributions, sponsor events, provide scholarships, and offer grants. They have valuable human resources in employees who are trained experts in fields like finance, marketing, law, medicine, logistics, and management. These employees, ranging in numbers from a few to tens of thousands, can serve as an army of volunteers, mentors, and board members, whose time and talents have immeasurable worth. Businesses also have physical assets to share, such as buildings, conference centers, office furniture, and trucks, which can also be equally valuable to nonprofits. Businesses are trending toward fully engaging in their communities with the trifecta of financial capital, human resources, and physical assets.

The Memphis-based, locally-owned office supply company, Yuletide Office Solutions, serves as a good example of how businesses can successfully integrate the trifecta. President and CEO, Chris Miller, has set the goal of giving over nine percent of net profits each year to charitable organizations. He's tied this goal into each employee's annual review by encouraging everyone to volunteer with at least two nonprofit events supported by the company. His team takes it a step further by reaching out to clients and vendors and leveraging those relationships to secure additional support for efforts, like food and holiday toy drives. The company then makes donating to these efforts more convenient by placing collection boxes at offices around the Mid-South and using their delivery trucks and drivers to collect the contributions. Yuletide's trucks are also utilized for local events like Meritan's Midnight Bike Ride to pick up bikers or volunteers who need a lift. (The ride, which is Meritan's signature community event, gives cyclers the opportunity to enjoy a 17-mile, non-competitive bike ride through the city by the light of the moon for the purpose of raising funds to provide resources for people with intellectual and developmental disabilities.)

Donny Granger, owner of Creation Studios Photography in Memphis, is yet another business person who has made effective use of the trifecta. He used his expertise and assets to help local professionals update their image and participate in a worthy community cause. Donny's offer of a FREE headshot session was accompanied by a simple request for participants to make a donation to the Memphis-Shelby County Law Enforcement Foundation's Fallen Officer Memorial fund. One hundred percent of the money went toward honoring the brave, local officers who sacrificed their lives in the line of duty while protecting the citizenry. By creatively leveraging his assets and aligning his artistic skillsets to a community cause, Donny succeeded in raising almost two thousand dollars for the Fallen Officer Memorial fund. Additionally, he generated extra publicity for his studio and increased his number of potential new clients. What a great win-win-win!

At Lipscomb & Pitts Insurance, we have a fully equipped conference center, complete with audio/visual capabilities and a full kitchen. When the space is not being utilized for business, we allow nonprofits and other groups to use the space and amenities free of charge. We also have an internal team who works with the nonprofits for scheduling, room tours, and equipment tutorials. Although this may be a comparatively small investment on our part, to the organizations we assist, it's a big help; and they're always very appreciative. The goodwill this simple cooperative effort builds not only strengthens our ties with the community but enables us to forge mutually beneficial partnerships with deserving nonprofits, as well.

I commend Chris Miller and Yuletide Office Solutions and Donny Granger at Creation Studios for setting fine examples of how businesses, regardless of their size or resources, can be instruments of progress and goodwill within their community. Creatively leveraging assets for the greater good can be less complicated than you would think. The benefits to be gained from even the smallest effort are almost always far greater than expected.

ENGAGING THE PUBLIC

Yet another trend in corporate philanthropy is engaging the public in the process of nominating or selecting nonprofits to receive donations. This is a win-win-win because the public is empowered to lobby support for deserving organizations that may not have appeared before on the radar screen of a corporation. These previously unnoticed nonprofits, then, become better positioned to receive much needed publicity and funding. The company, on the other hand, reaps the benefits of increased goodwill.

I offer as an example Monogram Foods' IMPACT10. Headquartered in Memphis, Monogram Foods is a leading manufacturer, distributor, and marketer of ready-to-eat jerky (beef, bacon, turkey, and chicken) and other meat snacks. It has five processing plants and over 1,800 employees throughout the country. To celebrate its 10 years in business, the company launched a public-driven charitable effort, IMPACT10.

As a part of this campaign, $150,000 was donated to 10 Mid-

South charities over 10 years. The public nominated the nonprofits via a website, impact10.com; then each week, for ten weeks, one organization was randomly selected. Subsequently, 10 charities each received $1,500 for 10 years! Some of the Mid-South charities who benefited included Harwood Center, HER Faith Ministries, New Day Children's Theatre, Ave Maria Home, and Boys and Girls Clubs of Crittenden County. Because the nonprofits were selected at random, no preference was given to one organization over another. As a result, some of the organizations selected were first time recipients of a Monogram Foods donation, which creates an opportunity for future growth and collaboration.

As a part of the process, Monogram Foods asked that the public nominators personally perform an act of kindness that would positively impact the community. The employees at Monogram Foods performed 10 acts of kindness, as well. Here the company and campaign engaged the public in both the financial and physical sides of philanthropy. That rates a "10" with me!

PHILANTHROPIC CAPITALISM AND THE ONE-FOR-ONE MODEL

Philanthropic capitalism, also known as philanthrocapitalism, is entrepreneurship at its finest. At its core, it's using business principles and processes to achieve philanthropic goals. Philanthrocapitalism is reshaping the way business leaders think, give, and work to make a more sustainable and magnified impact in the community. The perfect example of this is the one-for-one model, popularized by companies like TOMS Shoes, which donates a pair of shoes to a child in need for each pair purchased, and Warby Parker, which does the same with eyeglasses. Here in Memphis, we have companies like SoGiv and Agape North that also follow a one-for-one model. From the start, these companies have built purpose into their business model, so charitable costs are fixed and sustainable; they are not reliant on a percentage of profits that may or may not exist year after year.

In this manner, giving is automatic with each transaction, with each product and service sold. Gratification and impact are immediate. The advantage of this method, of course, is apparent – funding for charitable endeavors is secured systematically.

GIVING for GROWTH

In my view, this adds credence to the ideology that giving back is not just a random action but an act of PURPOSE.

Each "coin drop" in the charitable bank reinforces a person's or company's commitment to Giving for Growth!

This model affords a unique storyline that both customers and employees can feel good about and promote. It provides a competitive advantage with marketing and talent attraction and retention because there is a community benefit to each transaction. It becomes inspiring to know that every move made as an employee and every purchase made as a customer will ultimately help someone in need. Compare that to the feeling of not knowing if your daily actions on the job will yield any impact and it's easy to see which model is not only more sustainable, but more powerful, as well.

The one-for-one model may not be the right fit for every business; but the spirit and idea of the model is something that can be implemented in almost every industry across the board. Many companies are now automatically setting aside a percentage of each sale to fund charitable giving. These companies range from local restaurants to background screening and credit reporting agencies.

Other companies are using a variation similar to the "Round Up" programs that banks offer, where purchases automatically are rounded up to the next dollar amount and the rounded up change is deposited into a savings account. These companies, which range from clothing stores to repair shops, are not charging their customers more, but themselves setting aside the rounded up difference with each transaction. Again, the benefit is that with each transaction or new deal, charitable dollars are systematically allocated to benefit nonprofits.

In making the commitment to "Round Up" or contribute a set percentage of each transaction or promotion – whatever your product or service offering might be – you'll be amazed at how quickly the dollars add up and how great an impact your contribution will have on others. You'll also be raising the level of enthusiasm and motivation in your employees and co-workers.

Who wouldn't be energized knowing that your team's cooperative efforts will have a positive influence in your community, especially if you or your loved ones can directly or indirectly benefit from the improvement, too!

VOLUNTEERISM MUST BE TURNKEY

"Busy" is the new buzzword. Most of us have ever-increasing responsibilities with limited hours in a day to complete them. Time poverty is real, especially when you have young children! When our country's economy began to weaken, many of us found ourselves tasked with greater responsibilities and fewer resources. In spite of the slightly rebounding national economy, most companies are opting to remain lean, cross-train employees, and better utilize technology; thus, minimizing hiring. This decision is practical because, in general, employees have accepted multitasking and dual roles as the new norm for business. This new norm, however, has created new challenges, particularly for nonprofits.

Gone are the days when a nonprofit could operate efficiently with a small staff of volunteers who had the freedom and willingness to spend countless hours coordinating fundraising events or helping with programs and services. Nonprofits now must be extremely proactive in recruiting armies of volunteers and breaking down roles and responsibilities into bite-size, more manageable pieces. They are expanding board and committee options to include groups that exclusively meet during work hours and others that meet after work or on the weekends. With so much competition for volunteers' time, nonprofits have to make charitable work turnkey, in order to attract and engage needed support.

Understanding this trend is important because it illuminates the need for companies to take a leadership role in making volunteerism a part of their purpose. Companies can (and should) make it easy for their employees to become powerful forces for good. The win is BIG for everyone! Businesses reap the reward of increased community goodwill and visibility; employees are happier, more productive, and have a greater sense of team pride when workdays are infused with purpose; and our communities are enriched by the goodness inherent in giving back.

The concept of volunteerism is basic; and its implementation into the corporate world need not be problematic. We'll explore tactics to weave volunteerism into your routine and workday in future chapters, but there are many ways to engage employees while at the same time minimizing time lost to the company and maximizing the productivity of your team while on the job. As a quick example, we once combined our Lipscomb & Pitts Insurance Communications Department team meeting with a MIFA Meals on Wheels delivery. MIFA (mifa.org) is a Memphis-based nonprofit supporting the independence of vulnerable seniors and families in crisis through high-impact programs. One of their programs is Meals on Wheels, which provides hot, nutritious lunches for homebound senior citizens. Our team rode together to pick up hot and cold coolers that were packed with lunches and other healthy items, like milk and fruit, then conducted a strategy session in between making some very special deliveries. Along the way, we made a number of new friends who invited us into their homes to share stories, laughs, and quite a few hugs. In this manner, our normal hour and a half meeting was transformed into a moving and joyous experience that was also very productive.

The whole key to volunteering is to START – get involved! It's usually surprising how fast a volunteer program can take off and how BIG a difference can be made when people decide to roll up their sleeves, lead by example, and make volunteerism a priority.

Now that you've gained a better perspective of the trends in corporate philanthropy, I hope you're beginning to think of ways that YOU can infuse purpose and make volunteerism an integral part of your business's daily activities. The next step is to make those ideas reality. Let's move on to set the stage and then unfold the strategies and tactics for Giving for Growth.

THOUGHTS & ACTION STEPS

GIVING for GROWTH

Chapter Three

SETTING THE STAGE IN YOUR CAREER

Before delving into the strategies and tactics for Giving for Growth, let me restate that if our "community" – our neighborhoods, cities, states, and, ultimately, our nation – is ever going to be truly vibrant, then everyone must be actively involved in the effort. Each of us, regardless of our age or circumstances, needs to have pride and take ownership in being part of the process. Even when challenged by limited financial resources, we need not be deterred from achieving our goals. Remember, money is a great resource; but PEOPLE physically solve problems. By working cooperatively with others toward a worthy goal, individuals can achieve the impossible, just by taking small, simple, daily steps! Let's explore three ways giving back can get you ahead.

FIRST: ENRICHING YOUR PERSONAL STORY

As we've discussed, we live in a hyper-connected, technology-driven era where trust and community engagement are critical to corporate success. Thanks to social media and other platforms of connectivity, companies are moving from traditional "one-way" broadcasting toward interactive "two-way" conversations with team members, customers, and communities. The "one size fits all" mentality is being replaced with the expectation for individualization and customization. As consumers, we want it our way, right away! So, companies are looking for employees who understand this dynamic, who will embrace this heightened level of connectivity and collaboration; and also represent their brand with integrity out in the community.

For companies and individuals alike, it's now about conversations. It's about storytelling and engaging an audience that hopefully will share your story with others. As a result, some companies, like Nike, ask their employees to deliver presentations and quarterly updates without the use of PowerPoint. Individuals are shifting from bullet-point résumés to biographies that better reflect character and offer perspective, realizing it comes down to using their unique talents and story to stand out. Being engaged in the community enhances your personal story and gives you compelling experiences that are attractive to business leaders. In fact, having a community-focused storyline affords a distinct advantage for both a business and anyone searching for a job or trying to stand out in today's competitive workplace.

SECOND: EXPANDING YOUR SPHERE OF INFLUENCE

Ask most business leaders what's paramount outside of the well-being of their family and the success of their business and one of the top responses will be something related to "community engagement." Business leaders serve on nonprofit boards and understand the symbiotic relationship and role the community plays in their company's success, whether it's on an economic or intrinsic level. They realize that investing in education helps curb crime and creates a larger, more highly-skilled workforce. Talent development leads to economic growth and an improved quality of life; it can also generate a higher level of discretionary income. A higher level of discretionary income gives consumers the ability to purchase an increased number of goods and services; and this, of course, benefits the business.

Getting actively engaged in the community and with local nonprofits gives you the perfect platform for associating and finding common interests with business leaders. I know this from personal experience! It ties back to the truth that people provide opportunities for people. Your community service and volunteerism will expand your sphere of influence. It will allow you to meet and work with prominent business and community leaders, who can open doors of opportunity and also serve as powerful allies for making an even greater difference in the lives of others.

THIRD: ENHANCING YOUR LEADERSHIP SKILLS

Working with a nonprofit can help you sharpen your leadership skills and showcase your unique expertise. In the process of volunteering or leading a project, you are honing your skills, revealing your expertise, and developing a bond of trust with business leaders and the nonprofit. Keep in mind that nonprofits hire people, too; and what better place is there for them to look for new hires than within the rank of their valued volunteers?

Giving back is always the right thing to do! Some would argue that giving back should always be a selfless act; but no one can deny the existence of an inherent "return" value in giving ourselves to others. When people DO good, they FEEL good about themselves. This tends to give them a more positive attitude, which, in turn, boosts their confidence and heightens their motivation to accomplish tasks. When people grow personally because of these positive influences in their lives and when they are able to perform tasks more efficiently and effectively because of increased skills, everyone benefits! This is why weaving community engagement into your business routine is a good growth strategy. Using community engagement as an avenue for self-improvement, then, should be viewed in a positive light. Perhaps the following story will further illustrate this point.

HOW GIVING LEADS TO RECEIVING

Football legend, Herschel Walker, was our cityCURRENT guest speaker in April 2012. His presence attracted huge crowds; and his presentations inspired all in attendance. Part of his encouraging message focused on how giving back opened doors and led to opportunities that have yielded remarkable success in his business and personal life; so he would be pleased that I'm now sharing his story in this book to inspire you.

Herschel Walker was born in Wrightsville, Georgia, to a blue-collar family with seven children. As a child, he was overweight, dyslexic, and had a speech impediment. This caused him to be bullied by the kids and labeled "special" by his teachers. At an early age, however, Herschel made a commitment to take control of his life and proactively deal with these challenges. You might be familiar with the daily routine he subsequently developed: 2,500 sit-ups, 1,500 push-ups, and racing trains to improve his speed. Herschel went on to become the valedictorian of his high school class. On the football field, he broke records throughout his long career in high school, the NCAA, and the NFL.

Upon retiring from football, Walker parlayed skills developed and lessons learned on the field into a successful career as an author and entrepreneur. What started as a simple desire "to give a man a job" has expanded into an impressive corporate portfolio that includes Renaissance Man Foods, which supplies 250 million pounds of chicken for McDonald's globally; seven hospitals; a hotel linen company; promotional products; and a bakery. The total number of people employed exceeds 900!

Walker gives all the credit and glory for his success to God and his team; but his story reveals two noteworthy concepts that support my own philosophy of giving back. First is the power of helping someone and not expecting anything in return. Walker's mantra is "God looks at us and says, 'What have you done for someone else?' " Call it the "Butterfly Effect" or "Law of Attraction," but this altruistic mindset draws in people and creates genuine, powerful relationships that can, at some point in your life, help you – even when you had no expectation of that help. In Walker's case, most of his businesses were forged from relationships formed years ago by helping someone.

Second is the power of philanthropy. Walker automatically gives 15 percent of all profits from his businesses to charity. Money earned from his MMA (Mixed Martial Arts) events is donated to churches; and proceeds from his book are either donated or invested in his hospitals, which care for military veterans who need psychological help transitioning back into society after serving in combat zones. Some business owners may think Walker is foolish to give away so much money; but the more Walker gives, the more he seems to receive.

Building relationships while helping others offers people unlimited potential for personal and professional growth. It enhances our enjoyment of life; it encourages us to be better people (and citizens); it helps us improve our interpersonal and technical skills; and it empowers us with increased confidence in our ability to succeed, particularly when we see the positive effects our actions have when we lend a hand to lift up someone else.

THE POWER OF *REALATIONSHIPS*

Power is derived from either access to resources or influence. Resources like money afford you the ability to enjoy comforts and create opportunities for yourself and others in the community. For those who don't have a readily accessible stockpile of resources, though, there is another avenue for achieving your goals. In this interconnected, competitive world, influence and access to people – an audience – can be your ticket to success.

Companies are constantly seeking new ways to promote their goods and services; and they are willing to pay a premium to access an engaged, potentially brand-loyal audience. This marketing principle also applies to your personal life. The more people you know, the more expansive your potential reach. The deeper your relationship – the more your "audience" engages and trusts you – the more power you possess. This power can yield better career opportunities and higher salary options because, in today's corporate marketplace, the best jobs are found through personal referral networks.

When it comes to building your sphere of influence, you have at your disposal a variety of free tools like LinkedIn, Twitter, Facebook, YouTube, Instagram, and Periscope. These online sites have powerful business applications; and you can find numerous examples of individuals who have built successful careers utilizing their expertise to leverage these networks. Writing a blog is another way to showcase your talents and build an audience.

Face-to-face, personal connections, however, are by far the most effective means of building your network. Electronic networking and distributing your business cards at events may open a window of opportunity, but if you want to open a door of opportunity, that door hinges on your establishing REALationships. REALationships start with a selfless attitude and the genuine query, "What can I do to help you?" REALationships are forged over time and strengthened by commitments fulfilled, expectations exceeded, and trust unbroken. This is why volunteering is an ideal platform not only for giving back, but for establishing credibility with influential business leaders who care deeply about the community.

If you truly aspire to become a more powerful, influential force for good and achieve more success in your personal and professional life, you must purposefully work to build solid REALationships with those in your community. These REALationships will serve as the firm foundation on which you can build a lasting legacy of giving back. Once people truly know you, fully trust you, and readily think of you when they need help, you have attained a level of power that is certain to open doors of opportunity for you.

BEING "IN THE KNOW" ABOUT JOB OPPORTUNITIES AND TAKING INITIATIVE

Being "in the know" about good job opportunities and building a sphere of influence for career advancement also requires building REALationships. It ties back to the second of The Three Truths. For simplicity, keep in mind this more memorable maxim of bestselling author, Andy Andrews: "Opportunities come from people."

Leaders understand this fundamental truth. They know the importance of relationships and also understand that the success of their company is tied to the well-being of their community; and, therefore, they value those around them who strive to make a difference. If you're job-seeking, wanting a promotion, or needing to expand your influence, volunteering with nonprofits can give you the extra advantage you require to meet your objective. It strengthens your résumé, adds interest and depth to your unique story, and, of course, expands your network of people who know you and have the ability to provide new opportunities.

What you've just read in the preceding paragraph is part of the message we at cityCURRENT and Lipscomb & Pitts share with local college students every semester. After each of these student interactions, we tell students to reach out to us if they have questions, need help, or want to get more engaged in our community. Taking us up on this offer, however, is left to the students because, as in business and as in life, follow-up requires individual initiative. During the seven years we've hosted these events on college campuses, we've offered our open door to thousands of students. Are you surprised to learn that, in this seven-year period, only a handful of students took the initiative to follow up?

One of the students who reached out was Alton Cryer. He asked me to be his mentor; and I accepted. We started with quarterly lunches and progressed to days of shadowing. In the process, he met the rest of my team and started building a rapport with them. We quickly saw his sincere and warm personality, his inquisitiveness, and thirst for knowledge. We were amazed by his determination and grateful heart, as well. When Alton later asked for guidance in securing an internship, our staff immediately invited him to work at Lipscomb & Pitts Insurance. Alton had taken the time and made the effort to build a REALationship with me, my entire team, and many others in our agency, so it was an easy, natural next step to hire him as an intern. This is exactly how job opportunities are created and earned!

Alton exemplifies the type of person we look for in the workplace. He showed initiative in reaching out and following up. He worked hard – at two jobs – to put himself through college. Equally admirable, he allotted time to give back to his community through a mentoring program he started for helping youth and senior citizens. He always wore a smile and was quick to show appreciation. Alton has since completed his internship, graduated from the University of Memphis, and moved on to a full-time career; and he continues to grow his own nonprofit, STS Enterprise (STSenterprise.org), as well. He and I still remain close friends. If he were ever to need my help in the future, I hope to be there for him because he has earned my confidence, respect, and trust.

THE MOST EXPENSIVE THING IS TRUST

When making presentations, I frequently share with the audience this quote from DavesWordsofWisdom.com: "The most expensive thing in this world is TRUST! It can take YEARS to EARN and only a matter of SECONDS to LOSE." Trust serves as the bedrock for all strong, enduring relationships. This is why the foremost point in the Boy Scout Law is "A Scout is Trustworthy." What does being trustworthy mean? In the Boy Scout Handbook, the meaning is clear-cut and direct: "A Scout tells the truth. He is honest, and keeps his promises. People can depend on him."

Telling the truth, being honest, and keeping promises – these are the essential elements of building and maintaining trust in every relationship, be it personal, business, or community. Of late, it may seem that the importance of being trustworthy has diminished; but without trust we have no foundation to build upon and will not realize sustained success. Trust remains a top priority in people's lives, even if they are not always acting in a trustworthy manner. For businesses, establishing a workforce that is trustworthy has a multitude of benefits, including having a more positive image. Brands are, in fact, "promises" to maintain the highest level of quality in both goods and services being offered to its customers, its employees, and the community. I doubt any company could survive long, much less flourish, if customers, employees, and the community viewed it as untrustworthy.

Another facet of trust is dependability. How can you trust someone if you can't depend on him or her? Being dependable – like keeping promises – takes commitment, discipline, and sacrifice; but it's a personal and professional trait you can be proactive in building, day after day, through volunteerism. Establishing yourself as someone who is highly dependable makes developing the REALationships you desire much easier. Once you take the initiative to reach out to others and then commit yourself to a specific action, it is imperative that you sustain those REALationships by always being dependable. Someone recently pointed out to me that "dependability" is usually seen as a single word; but it's actually the conjoining of two equally important words, "depend" and "ability." Unless others can depend on you to do something, your ability to do it becomes inconsequential. How is this relevant to getting ahead? Two people have equal ability to do an important job. One person is dependable, the other is not. Whom would you trust and choose for the job?

CHARACTER ALWAYS COUNTS

Remember the Golden Rule, "Do unto others as you would have them do unto you"? As children, my brother and I often heard our parents remind us of this Christian code of conduct; and although the reminder was sometimes overemphasized, it served an admirable purpose. It taught us to be thoughtful of others and behave in a courteous manner. Now, as a parent myself, I see the wisdom of my mother's and father's use of the Golden Rule as a teaching tool. My wife and I utilize it, too, not just to encourage our sons to behave properly, but to help them understand the importance of compassion, consideration, and character.

In my view, the Golden Rule is synonymous with good sportsmanship – and the graceful acceptance of defeat. In the game of life, sometimes we win; sometimes we lose. The one constant in life, however, must be our character. Strength of character transcends workplace performance because it empowers people to make ethical decisions when necessary. Although traditional, faith-based moral values like honesty, trust, and integrity may often be trivialized by some segments of our society, these character traits are still highly valued by business leaders, particularly those who are committed to giving back. Character ALWAYS counts.

Character in your career means following the Golden Rule and doing what is right, even when no one is watching. Let's assume you are a courier making a delivery at a residence. You notice a heavy stream of water flowing down the driveway of the home. What would you do? Would you ignore the problem to keep to your delivery schedule; or would you drive to the homeowner's business to inform that person of what was happening at the residence? If you chose the latter action, you would have made the same ethical and courteous decision as FedEx courier, Steve Simpson. By following the Golden Rule, Steve helped the homeowner save his family's house from flooding. When the family expressed their gratitude to Steve on Facebook, the story quickly made its way up to the very top of FedEx Corporation's leadership!

Employers endeavor to hire ethical people who will work hard, treat co-workers and customers with respect, take responsibility, lead by example, and do what is right. If you commit yourself to Giving for Growth, you must strive to give your very best to every endeavor, every day, so the legacy you leave will be one of excellence. In the words of Dr. Bertice Berry, "Your legacy isn't what you leave when you die; it's what other people say about you when you leave the room." What do you want people to say about you?

BECOMING A CATALYST BEGINS WITH DEFINED PURPOSE

One day as I was having lunch with faculty members from a local university, the conversation turned to entrepreneurship and the role higher education plays in economic development. One of the topics of discussion was how schools could be more proactive in not only equipping graduates with the skills necessary to succeed in today's marketplace, but how they could help enhance the quality of life for all Mid-South citizens. The dialog was thought-provoking. The challenge it raised might at first seem impossible; but, from my experience, viable solutions can always be found when people take purposeful action to help others. If educational institutions, graduates, and entrepreneurs are to become community catalysts, it begins with how purpose is defined. I think you'll find the following story proves my point.

Veronika Scott, CEO and founder of The Empowerment Plan, was a product design student in Detroit when she was challenged with a class assignment to create a product that would fulfill a community need. Her idea was to help homeless individuals by designing a coat that converts into a sleeping bag at night and an over-the-shoulder bag when not in use. What started as a product, however, quickly transformed into a mission when one of the homeless women stated the obvious: "We don't need coats; we need jobs!"

Established in 2011, The Empowerment Plan (EmpowermentPlan. org) employs 20 previously homeless men and women and pays a living wage for them to manufacture the coats. They're dedicated to serving the homeless community by distributing coats free of charge to these people through partnerships with outreach organizations around the nation. Thus far, over 9,000 coats have been made and 6,500 are planned for production this year.

Veronika Scott's epiphany came when purpose was defined not by providing the coat, but by educating, employing, and empowering homeless people to create better lives for themselves.

I applaud Veronika for thinking BIG, taking purposeful steps to help others, and serving as the SPARK who ignites others to dream big, too. In addition, I commend her teacher for creating the opportunity for students like Veronika to become actively engaged in giving back to their community. What Veronika was able to accomplish from a project she, as a student, created because of an assignment by her teacher is a wonderful testimony to the power of giving back.

Learning to give back is a valuable life lesson! It can – and should – be "taught" everywhere in our communities: our schools, our colleges, our churches, our entrepreneurial incubators, our businesses, and our homes. It's imperative that we challenge individuals to become problem solvers focused on confronting issues in our neighborhoods and developing products and services that serve community needs. Likewise, we must shift our competitive focus to job creation and building civic wealth. If a rising tide lifts all ships, then let's define our purpose as that tide, so our actions will uplift all.

THREE DAILY STEPS

The phrase, "Movements start with small actions," applies as much to your personal life as to community efforts.

Other than winning a multi-million-dollar lottery, there simply is no such thing as an overnight success. We may witness a singer winning a contest on national television or an actor making it big with his or her first film; but what we almost never observe are the years of hard work, training, and sacrifice that goes into preparing for that "visible" success. Every experience we have in life (even those that might seem insignificant or unduly challenging at the time) prepares us for what lies ahead. These experiences also help us develop our skills and character, refine our approach and expectations, and build our confidence and faith.

As I mentioned in the Prelude, when I was in college, I pursued multiple "dreams" but knew I must still maintain my high academic standing for scholarships. It was definitely a challenge juggling all these responsibilities and still finding time to progress in the things I was even more passionate about, such as music and acting. Consequently, I committed to doing at least three things each day that would generate momentum for my passions. The steps could be small, like writing lyrics to a song or meeting someone new who might be interested in my music or who I could invite to a future performance; but I would not go to sleep until three steps were taken each day.

Over the years, this commitment to three daily steps has made a tremendous difference in my life; and the process can do the same for you in moving your community and your career forward. Giving back and making a difference does not have to be expensive or overly time consuming. Sending a note of encouragement, donating blood, opening the door for someone, mentoring or tutoring youth, picking up trash, donating clothes or toys, or just offering a compliment can suffice.

To close this chapter, I'm challenging you to accept my "Mission: Possible." For the next week, commit to doing three things (no matter how small) each day that will move your life or your community forward. If, by the end of the week, you've found this mission "doable," repeat the process for another week. When, by the end of the second week, you find this mission is "growing" on you (and perhaps others, if you've challenged them as well), accept the fact that you're hooked on giving back; and keep moving forward!

Fitting my "Three-Step" program into your daily routine can be easier than you think; and it can also be fun and rewarding. Once you've established the unconscious habit of giving back, I'm confident that you'll be reaping many of the tangible and intangible benefits to be derived from making a difference in someone else's life, including your own! You will be amazed, too, by the tidal wave of GOOD you'll have generated when you reflect on this experience in the future!

THOUGHTS & ACTION STEPS

GIVING for GROWTH

Chapter Four

SETTING THE STAGE PERSONAL

Do you know someone who is highly successful career-wise but is struggling in his or her personal life? Success in business is an impressive manifestation of our hard work, continuous improvement, and dedication; but who we are as a person with our values, attitude, and integrity for example, ultimately has a greater impact on our life and career than any individual business achievements. So, we must be careful not to devote all of our time and energy to building our careers, consequently neglecting growth in our personal lives. In actuality, who we are as a person has everything to do with determining our level of professional success.

One of the hardest lessons learned by those who are transitioning from college to career is the realization that their personal and professional brands are intertwined. In today's hyper-connected world, everybody's lives and opinions are more public than ever. Gone are the days of "It's not personal; it's just business." Life is personal and ALL about relationships; and so is business today! Look on any social media platform and you'll readily find rants and raves for anything and everything, including customer and employee interactions with your business. While it may be hard to ascertain dollars gained or lost from individuals sharing experiences on social media, one thing is for certain: people are talking!

GIVING for GROWTH

Companies invest huge amounts of time, effort, and money into training and equipping employees and building and maintaining their reputation in the community. What's the reason behind so great an investment? *Forbes* publisher, Rich Karlgaard, identifies it as an important factor he calls "The Soft Edge," which includes variables like trust, smarts, teamwork, taste, and story. "The Soft Edge" incorporates social impact and philanthropy and allows an organization to find brand differentiation. Since a company's brand is perceived as a promise and a culmination of experiences, it requires vigilant safeguarding by its stewards, the employees.

Safeguarding a company's brand can come in a variety of forms, from obvious to subtle. The latter approach was used by a local nonprofit that was selling T-shirts. They stated they'd be proud for us to wear the shirts out in the community; but they jokingly added that they'd prefer we change out of them if we were headed anywhere "inappropriate." Although their comment came across as a joke, the truth behind it is people notice.

Here's another example that helps drive home my point. I had lunch with a business owner who shared an interesting story. He was watching his nephew's ballgame; and when the boy's team went to make a play, a man in the crowd shouted, "Take him out! Break his leg!" The business owner recognized the shouter as an employee of a vendor his company used; so the next day he discontinued that relationship. While this may seem extreme to some people, the business owner's reasoning was understandable. The shouter's personal conduct – even outside the realm of business – was perceived as a reflection of the employee's professional character and of his employer's, as well. (Remember my earlier statement, Character ALWAYS counts?)

Accepting the reality that the world IS always watching and that your personal actions DO impact professional opportunities can go a l-o-n-g way in helping you make better decisions for your life, both personally and professionally. Striving each day to make every aspect of your life positive encourages you to move forward and to grow into a person whose life reflects multi-faceted success. If you accepted my "Mission: Possible" challenge in the last chapter, you've already made a positive decision for your personal growth. Make another by completing the entire challenge. You have nothing to lose and everything to gain. That's how giving back can get you ahead!

ATTITUDE IS A SELF-FULFILLING PROPHECY

When I was living in Los Angeles, I had the privilege of working with Merv Griffin, running his celebrity tennis tournaments. This was definitely an amazing experience; and it paved the way for many friendships and professional opportunities that have grown over the years. As a mentor, Griffin taught me much about succeeding in life and business. One day, just in passing, I asked him the key to success. His answer was succinct: attitude.

Attitude is a self-fulfilling prophecy. Like tossing a free throw in basketball or making a serve in tennis, we control our every action, and reaction. Like our careers and our personal lives, we mold our attitudes, day by day. Our attitude, of course, affects the way we think and feel about ourselves and others, and how we perceive challenges and opportunities. Consequently, our attitude ultimately dictates our behavior.

Griffin understood that in life and business, leadership and success depend on belief and people. In order to accomplish something of real magnitude, it takes teamwork. Sports teams, corporations, nonprofits, schools, governments, and even entrepreneurs all rely on collaboration to achieve success. Aristotle's famous assertion, "The whole is greater than the sum of its parts," rings true even today. Teamwork creates amazing synergy; it makes 1 + 1 = 3. Griffin knew well that people are the real vehicles for new opportunities, the inspirations for ideas and innovation, and the physical hands that build and create.

The synergistic collaboration that drives success, however, deadlocks with negative energy. Think of your office or of family and friends and how one bad attitude instantly alters the chemistry and relationship. No one enjoys associating with someone who has a negative attitude. A negative attitude divides and discourages. On the other hand, a positive attitude acts as a magnet; and what it will attract is people, people who can afford you more opportunities in life and who can help you build and create something special. A famous proverb states this in another, more memorable way, "You can catch more flies with honey than with vinegar." Translated by Wiktionary.org, this proverb describes how "It's easier to persuade others with polite requests and a positive attitude than with rude demands and negativity." Whether you see it like a "magnet" or "honey," make sure to be aware of and take responsibility for the attitude you bring into your home and office each and every day.

A CITY THAT CARES

The importance of having a positive attitude is not limited to your home and office, though; attitude plays a defining role in how we view our community, choose to act and react, and interact with others everywhere we go. There's a parable of a man standing in line who is met by someone new to town. The newcomer asks, "What's this city like?" The man replies, "What was it like where you came from?" The newcomer says, "It was miserable; there wasn't much to do." The man solemnly states, "It will be the same here." Later that day, the man is met by a different newcomer, who asks him the same question, "What's this city like?" The man replies, "What was it like where you came from?" The second newcomer says, "It was beautiful; I had many friends and things to do." The man smiles and offers, "It will be the same here."

Indeed, attitude is a powerful determinant for how we view our community and ourselves. Our attitude is the lens that clarifies or distorts our perspectives, happiness, and civic pride. This lens, sometimes called our "terministic lens," uses past experience to shape the way we view the world. Consider a concert where all of the attendees listen to the same band and set of songs. Each attendee walks in with different preconceived expectations and attitudes and so, afterward when you ask for feedback, it varies widely.

My family and I have lived in the Mid-South for eight years now and we love it! We love it so much that we invested into my company's ownership, so we're here to stay. My lens is that of endless opportunity and caring citizens who have become good friends.

In fact, I recently sat down with a friend who has been traveling to Memphis for some time and just made an offer on a home here.

He lost his driver's license and when he tried to rent a car at the airport, he was denied due to policy. A caring employee, who knew him, found a solution. The employee gave him his personal car while the employee rented one for the week, stating, "I've got your back." One person's attitude and actions can make a difference! A positive attitude can transcend to permeate a city! Personally, I love living in a city that has my back – a city that cares!

THE POWER OF WORDS

If attitude is a self-fulfilling prophecy and an engine driving our ability to connect and achieve success, words are the wheels that carry us and quickly move us forward or backward. With this in mind, I'm going to borrow a lesson from a Sunday sermon by Pastor James Lewis at DeSoto Hills Baptist Church. The Message had as its base Ephesians 5:1-7. Obviously, our pastor's intent was for us to focus on our spirituality and our moral compass; but I found his sermon to be a perfect fit for extending our discussion on attitude and describing how words correlate to a person's ability to make a difference.

Although people physically solve problems, it takes a collaborative effort to affect change. An individual can give and do much; but when individuals combine forces to motivate others, an exponential effect occurs. If one person inspires three individuals, who then each engage three others, who also do the same, think of the magnitude that impact will make. Thousands of volunteers could be mobilized!

The power of our human connectivity, however, is directly related to our level of positive energy. As we've discussed, negative energy only serves to divide and repel people, while, on the other hand, positive energy electrifies others and ignites a fire of enthusiasm for your cause. People who are the most successful in their careers and their personal lives are those who maintain a positive attitude, regardless of the challenges they face. Having a "can do" attitude empowers individuals with a herculean strength that enables them to surmount even the highest obstacle. Having a positive attitude is a personal choice, one only YOU can make.

Attitude, however, is not the only thing you should be mindful of in order to maximize your potential for success. Your words are powerful; they can affect your career, your reputation, and your ability to create change. As my pastor sagely stated in that sermon, "Sticks and stones bruise temporarily; words will forever help or hurt you." Choose your words wisely, then, and always be attentive to how and where you speak them. People notice; people listen; people talk.

With the proliferation of social media, word travels quickly. Even with disclaimers like "Opinions are my own," your personal brand is tied to your professional brand. It's tempting, especially in an emotionally-heightened state, to express thoughts and opinions without proper context or knowing the whole story. How can anything positive ever come from your texting, emailing, or speaking negative statements in the heat of anger? Those negative words will come back to haunt you. They can damage your personal and professional reputation; destroy valuable relationships; and even cost you your position or your job. It just makes good sense (and cents) to view all your interactions as extensions of your "personally professional" brand.

Words have immense power; but actions speak louder than words, especially when it comes to building your credibility. Credibility comes from your willingness to roll up your sleeves, dig in, and be a part of the solution. Credibility builds trust and inspires others to follow you; but you must lead by example – and always endeavor to be the right example. If you want to make a real difference in your life and in your surroundings, you'll need to make it your daily mission to focus on positive energy, be mindful of your words, and build credibility with your actions by working with and helping the people in your community.

ENCOURAGING GOOD DEEDS

I had the pleasure of sitting in on a class at the University of Memphis that was taught by the Hollywood Film Director, Screenwriter, and Producer, Tom Shadyac. Here in Memphis, Tom has become well-loved for his generosity. He donates his time and services to teach the class, feeds his students, and gives each of them a bicycle to remind them to have fun in life. He gives local elementary school kids new bikes, as well.

His goal is to teach students to give to society what they expect to receive from it – kindness, happiness, consideration, goodwill, and prosperity.

One of the videos Shadyac played in class that day was the "People for Good 'Babies' 60 second TV Commercial." If you watch this on YouTube, you will see sweet, innocent faces of babies paired with sour tags like "slams doors in people's faces" and "rude to neighbors." The commercial serves as an effective reminder that no one is born "bad." All along our journey in life, we are molded by parents, family, teachers, mentors, friends, and faith – and, of course, media and other social influencers. The behaviors and beliefs that we parents and leaders choose to instill in our children and those whom we lead will become part of our living legacy. What values will you choose to encourage? Keep in mind, there is a big difference between "You have to BE the best" and "You have to DO your best," especially when it comes to sportsmanship.

Every one of us is a leader in some way; and good leaders realize that encouragement can be a very effective tool for reinforcing positive behavior. My older son was beaming after my wife showed him a complimentary email from his teacher, recognizing his helpfulness to other students. Now he wants to arrive at school even earlier to help more. Organizations like JIFF (jiffyouth.org) and tnAchieves (tnachieves.org) have attained remarkable success with youth because volunteers mentor, share their time, and perform simple acts of support like sending text messages of encouragement. If someone took the time to send you words of encouragement or a note of thanks for something you did, how did their words make you feel? These gestures are all forms of giving back and creating positive outcomes.

One of my friends committed himself to doing three daily steps and has made it a point to write at least one handwritten letter each day, thanking someone for a job well done or a random act of kindness. Over the last three years, this commitment has afforded him the opportunity to brighten the day of more than 700 individuals; but my friend would be the first to say that his day was illuminated just as much, if not more, because he smiles at the end of each letter written. Also, I think it's important to add that my friend has received many thank you notes in return from individuals who, unbeknownst by my friend at the time, were facing a challenge, or feeling down or unnoticed at the office, yet felt inspired after receiving his kind note. So, what can you do to encourage someone each and every day?

A RESOLUTION OF RECOGNITION

Several years ago, I resolved to be more intentional in picking up litter. My resolution included a personal goal of encouraging others to volunteer in this effort. I laugh about this now because little did I know, at that time, that we would later be bringing in Chad Pregracke of Living Lands & Waters as a guest speaker with cityCURRENT. Pregracke has made it his life's work to clean up the Mississippi River. In the past 15 years, he and his team of volunteers have helped pull more than 67,000 tires from U.S. waterways; and that's just scratching the surface.

So, I had no idea that, as a result of Pregracke's presentation, we would be teaming with the University of Memphis, Memphis City Beautiful Commission, and River Warriors (led by Colton Cockrum) to help clean up McKellar Lake. McKellar Lake, which was an important part of Memphis' social life and packed with boats and festivities back in the 1950s and 1960s, had lost its luster and become heavily polluted over the years. I'm proud to say, though, that McKellar Lake now looks much better and that over the last four years, thousands of volunteers have participated in the cleanup effort. Together we've removed over 90,000 pounds of trash from that lake!

My most recent resolution is to be more intentional with positive affirmation and in recognizing the daily efforts of the people closest to me in my life. Admittedly, I move at light speed and have way too many thoughts constantly bouncing off each other; sometimes I get sidetracked and don't take time to notice the successes of those around me, including my wife and children. By resolving to recognize and affirm the efforts of at least one person a day, I'm purposefully working toward becoming a better husband, father, friend, co-worker, and leader.

I share this resolution with the hope it will impact you in a similar way as the "Butterfly Effect," where one good deed sets in motion a wave of positive actions. Movements start with small actions, like a simple word of praise. An associate of mine once commented that "If you want to set the tone for an amazing evening with your family, make sure to walk through the door with a smile on your face and the enthusiasm to immediately tell each one how much you love and appreciate them." How much simpler can giving back be? Resolve, right now, to take a small step toward giving back to others. Set the "Butterfly Effect" in motion today! If you give an individual you know a compliment or say "thanks" to someone, even a stranger, you can spread happiness throughout your community.

This same idea of recognition and appreciation carries over to those who serve our country and safeguard our freedoms. My younger brother, Jeff, always wanted to be in the military. Growing up, he would watch war movies, read history books, talk with veterans, and play games that tested skill and strategy. He was laser focused on community service and helping others in need. Our family was understandably proud of him when he became an Eagle Scout and also when he became a U.S. Marine.

Now, seventeen years later, Jeff has served numerous tours of combat duty and has experienced circumstances similar to the movie, *Saving Private Ryan*. He doesn't talk readily about his missions; but thanks to a cityCURRENT guest speaker, who was a former Navy SEAL, I caught a glimpse of Jeff's reality. I eavesdropped as my brother and the speaker shared war stories about ambushes and losing friends, the importance of candy bars for building trust between them and the Afghan children, and the necessity of towelettes for staying clean. That day, I gained a new perspective on what sacrifice truly means.

Jeff still proudly serves in the military and, as you'd expect, continues to help others in need. He helped coordinate the Marine's relief efforts in Nepal after the earthquake there earlier this year; and he works tirelessly with military personnel in Thailand, Guam, South Korea, and the Philippines, helping them train to respond to similar disasters or attacks. Since Jeff is currently stationed overseas, I stay in touch with him, his wife Rachel, and their adorable kids, Thomas and Harper, through Facebook.

I also enjoy seeing pictures of other family members, friends, and their relatives, who serve in our military and as first responders. Many friends here in the Mid-South are police officers and firefighters. They are neighbors, parents, coaches, church leaders, and selfless civic servants. They are brave individuals, who give back and help those in need. They risk their lives to deal with the worst in life so we can enjoy the best. They are mothers and fathers, with loved ones and children waiting anxiously for their return home.

My gratitude goes out to all the brave men and women who protect our freedoms every day. I make it a priority to recognize and thank our public servants as often as I see them. I hope you will do the same. It is the least I can do for my brother and for all who faithfully serve our city and nation.

WHAT IT MEANS TO BE AN UPSTANDER

I remember a day when my parents were rushing to get me and my brother ready for a tennis tournament. Normally, the two of us got along great; but on this particular morning, we were at odds. My brother tried to get in the car on the side I was sitting; and he attempted to step over my outstretched legs. I made no effort to move my legs; so he tripped and fell. That did not please my parents. As we both were being chastised for agitating each other, I tried to proclaim my innocence. It was then that my father shared a life lesson that has stuck with me ever since: If you aren't part of the solution, you're part of the problem.

That could seem a harsh statement; but the underlying truth is sound. If you see a need or challenge in the community and opt to be a bystander, then the problem will remain unresolved (and probably will become bigger). People find it much easier to complain or create an excuse to do nothing rather than take any action to remedy the situation. It's time to re-ignite that good old-fashioned American "can do" attitude on which our country was built.

In essence, this is what Facing History and Ourselves (facinghistory.org) has been working to do. The organization, founded in 1976 in Brookline, Massachusetts, reaches nearly three million students yearly via a network of more than 90,000 educators. They have educational partnerships around the world, including Northern Ireland, South Africa, and China, and ten offices here in the United States. The organization impacts over 200,000 middle and high school students in the greater Memphis area and helps these students make the essential connection between history and the moral choices they confront in their own lives today. Facing History and Ourselves recognized a need; and they chose to act on that need by becoming engaged. Their goal is to develop responsible citizens, people who can, and will, step forward to be part of the solution for needs that arise in their community. Instead of being "bystanders," Facing History and Ourselves wants their alumni to be "upstanders."

Upstanders are people who stand up for what is right and choose to use their resources to help others and strengthen our cities. Upstanders intentionally share positives and look for ways to support, lift, and bring people together. Every city, business, and individual will face difficult and challenging times; but the fortitude to transcend these difficulties and challenges will come from upstanders, local "heroes" who are willing to step up, take action, and find solutions to the problems. Every community needs more upstanders. Will you be one?

Part of being an upstander is becoming a champion for your community. A few years ago, Facing History and Ourselves hosted a free public exhibition, *Choosing to Participate*. The event was held at the Benjamin L. Hooks Central Library in Memphis. *Choosing to Participate* is part of a global initiative encouraging young people and adults to explore the question, "What does it mean to be a citizen in a democracy?" The exhibition challenged visitors to realize that our choices matter – to ourselves, our community, and our world.

Visitors viewed four multimedia installations about people and communities whose stories illustrated how courage, initiative, and compassion are necessary to protect democracy. One of the exhibits was "Not in Our Town," which told the story of how citizens in Billings, Montana, came together to fight a series of hate crimes. Homes and property were being vandalized; racist literature was being found around town; church services were being disrupted; the home of a Native American family was spray painted; and a brick was thrown through the window of a Jewish family's home. Law enforcement, civic leaders, faith groups, citizen activists, and local media outlets all came together and created a very powerful force and message: "Not in our town!" The local paper printed a menorah and encouraged everyone to post them in their windows; and the citizens took action. Business leaders and residents, regardless of their religious beliefs, banded together and posted the menorahs in the windows of their offices and homes to show solidarity. Ultimately, they were successful in kicking those responsible out of their city.

We have the same ability to create change and to stand proudly for our own cities, taking action and taking responsible control of the safety and beauty of our neighborhoods. To do so, though, we have to come together and see ourselves as upstanders and community champions. Once we do this, the way we interact with others, the way we talk about and celebrate our community, and the way we take action will cause us to become catalysts for positive change! So, I ask again, Will you be an upstander? Will you be a community champion?

LEGACY IS NOT DEFINED BY AGE

In our lifetime we will experience the loss of loved ones and people of great value in our personal and professional lives. With each life, whether intentional or not, a legacy is left behind for us to cherish and preserve. At one point, we were able to watch and benefit from the experiences that our loved ones and colleagues created with us and others; and we learned from their advice and stories, assistance, and encouragement. Their legacy, those traditions and memories, are now the very things we strive to pass along to future generations.

The amazing thing about legacy, though, is that it is not defined by age. We can create and enjoy our legacy now, so the memories we share, traditions we form, and lessons we impart create a tidal wave of blessings that will continue to grow long after we're gone. This type of legacy has nothing to do with money and everything to do with love and compassion. On a personal level, it's the time spent with family and friends or the open door policy of my parents;

on a professional level, it's how you mold your career and treat others in and outside of the workplace. Legacy encompasses every interaction with people and how you made them feel.

Gerold Blum, the younger brother of my former co-worker, Nicole McGlaughlin, was a champion of our Samaritan's Feet Shoe Distributions, always looking forward to not only washing the feet of our city's youth and giving them new socks and shoes, but recruiting family and friends to experience the joy of giving, as well. I was fortunate to see how Gerold could light up a room with his smile and how he made it a point to talk to everyone in the room, in order to lift their spirits. Gerold was an athlete and played football for Saint Benedict High School at Auburndale, where he graduated in 2013. He was also a standout cadet in the University of Memphis Army ROTC program, where he was the only freshman on the Ranger Team. Sadly, due to a rare heart condition, he was only 18 when his heart stopped beating and he left this world peacefully in his sleep.

Gerold's memorial services revealed the impact he had on THOUSANDS of people, not only as a talented, Godly young man with a bright future, but as someone who took the time to give back and care for others. He once saved the life of a friend by reaching out when times were tough and not letting his friend off easy, when the friend's response was "Nothing's the matter." He mobilized his friends to make a difference and Gerold made it a priority to be there when his mother battled breast cancer and his family needed him most. This is Gerold's legacy; and it will forever live on in the hearts of those who knew and loved him. It's only fitting that the University of Memphis Army ROTC program now celebrates Gerold's memory with an annual Gerold Blum Memorial 5k benefiting The American Heart Association.

Envision the legacy you want to leave behind. Think of your family and those who matter most; but then consider where you can reach out with your time and talents to touch others. It can be something simple like reading to kids at a school; but find something that requires you to give of yourself. Create traditions with your family and co-workers that incorporate a higher purpose of giving back. Then, make it a priority to record your experiences and stories, so these moments can be shared with others and future generations.

It's powerful knowing the legacy you live will become the legacy you leave.

Once again, consider the words of Dr. Bertice Berry, "Your legacy isn't what you leave when you die; it's what other people say about you when you leave the room." I love that quote because it's so simple and true. The length of our life is a blessing; but the quality of our life is our legacy. Indeed, we're creating our legacy with every interaction, so let's give every one our all and make the most of every moment!

THERE'S NO SILVER BULLET

Pursuing an idea or passion is like having a child. You pour your heart and soul, along with countless hours, into nurturing, developing, and growing a concept into something special. Along the way, you experience exhilarating highs, embarrassing lows, and lessons learned that build strength, character, and leadership. Parenting a child takes COMPLETE dedication and life-long, hard work. This parallels the foundation for building a life.

While we are obsessed with immediate gratification and global connectivity, patience is still an important virtue. There simply is no such thing as an overnight success. Almost every leader I have worked with or interviewed has concurred that a range of five to seven years is the typical amount of time to truly create impact, value, and sustainability with a new idea, product or program. I mention this because, almost each week, I work with individuals and organizations that have ambitious ideas and goals, yet expectations of instant results. The game plan tends to follow this basic progression: 1) Write a plan, 2) Raise money, 3) Build the business, website, or program, and 4) Watch it take off! My initial response is always "What are you doing now to bring this plan to life?"

One of my favorite phrases is "Think BIG, start small, and act NOW!" It aligns with my mindset of doing three simple things each day to move forward. Action creates clarity; and success lies in the flawless execution of the smallest details that create rewarding experiences. Adding a patient outlook to the equation is liberating because you're not searching for silver bullets. You already have the keys to long-term personal success; and you can start immediately.

Now that you've learned about The Three Truths, Trends in Corporate Philanthropy, and Setting the Stage in your Career and Personal Life, you're ready to move on to the strategies and tactics that will help you realize your dreams while helping others. These are the very blueprints and concepts I use in my life and the guidelines we employ for our efforts with cityCURRENT. In many cases, you'll see that we work backward. First, we determine where we want to go; then we devise a detailed plan for how to get there, i.e. who we need to meet and work with along the way. Beginning with the end in mind, then breaking it down into the individual steps and potential partners and influencers we'll need to attract helps our team find the heart, mission alignment, and connection points in the community.

Understand, though, that everything I've shared up to this point is extremely important because without the proper attitude and mindset, without being authentic and trustworthy, these strategies and tactics will be inconsequential. Giving for Growth means first opening your heart to serving others! Doing so enables you to incorporate the following tactics effectually, thereby maximizing the potential of success for your actions and efforts. Now that we've gotten to the "heart" of this matter, let's move forward!

GIVING for GROWTH

THOUGHTS & ACTION STEPS

GIVING for GROWTH

Chapter Five

TACTICS FOR GROWTH: CORPORATE

CREATE A COMMUNITY CALLING CARD

Every business needs a Community Calling Card. As you're seeing throughout this book, the marketing basics of a sleek logo, catchy slogan, polished advertising, and online presence now includes having a "cause" or purpose that transcends business and focuses on community. Consumers not only want to see corporate America physically engaged in helping and uplifting our citizens and neighborhoods, they fully expect it! Consumers and employees want to see the heart of a company; and, as Tom Shadyac has noted, they're deciding where to work and what to purchase based on "love."

Meeting this expectation goes beyond financial engagement like nonprofit contributions and sponsorships. It requires strategically aligning efforts with specific causes and adopting them as a part of your corporate mission. Once you fully embrace and adopt a nonprofit or cause, it can become your Community Calling Card. Just like a business card, your Community Calling Card is how your company will be recognized in your hometown and beyond. Over time, it will become one of your strongest differentiators, outside of products and services, because it proactively builds trust.

Think of your Community Calling Card as an opportunity for physically serving and engaging the community in a meaningful way. One of our Community Calling Cards with cityCURRENT is our Samaritan's Feet Shoe Distributions. Samaritan's Feet (samaritansfeet.org) is a nonprofit that works in over 75 countries to provide new shoes to the 1.5 billion people worldwide who currently face foot-born infection and diseases. To date, the organization has distributed more than 6.5 million shoes; but the most heart-warming part is that volunteers wash the feet of the recipients and share love and prayers for a bright future.

We've hosted Samaritan's Feet Shoe Distributions in Memphis since 2010 and have served thousands of youth, thanks to many partners and volunteers. As a team, we work to underwrite the cost and organize the event, then invite the community to participate for free. It's a moving experience when both the kids and volunteers walk out saying it was the best day of their lives. Adopting Samaritan's Feet gives our company a higher purpose and a calling card that engages our community. The events are a huge source of pride for our cityCURRENT team and have become both a fun, recognizable part of our efforts, as well as one of the "must attend" volunteer events of the year. You can create this same Community Calling Card in your hometown by teaming up with Samaritan's Feet or aligning with a local nonprofit to create a unique event that both draws people in and gives back to help your community. Just imagine how much we could uplift our cities and country if each company in the Mid-South and across America would adopt a nonprofit and create a Community Calling Card.

ENGAGE EMPLOYEES TO CREATE WIN[3]

As we discussed in Chapter Two, corporate philanthropy is now focused on engagement and creating support systems for employees so they can interact more easily with the community and donate their time, talents, and leadership. Consumers are looking to corporate America to be "upstanders," who find and deliver solutions for local needs. They are expecting corporations to be physically involved within their communities. Consequently, community engagement has become a core component of corporate sustainability.

You've seen me use the term a few times already, but for business executives, the objective is to create win³ (win-win-win) scenarios – opportunities where their company, employees, and community benefit simultaneously. To create win³ scenarios, leaders must provide their workforce with encouragement, freedom, and support to make a "hands on" impact. In an era where employees are working long hours and facing time poverty, companies can incentivize their teams in the following ways.

Allow employees to modify their work schedule. Many volunteer opportunities, such as reading to kids at a preschool in the morning or tutoring youth after school, fit in a workday; so allowing employees to adjust their schedules accordingly is a practical solution. Companies can allow employees to shift their schedules forward or backward so no time is lost or any deficit in hours can be made up another day. For example, an employee could volunteer to deliver meals to senior citizens from 8:30 AM to 9:30 AM and be back at the office by 10:00 AM; or an individual could leave early – like at 3:30 PM – to help students with homework from 4:00 PM to 5:00 PM, thus ending their workday at a normal time. Additionally, the employee's volunteer time can be credited toward a monthly or annual allotment of hours designated by the company. As another option, corporations can provide a certain amount of time each month that can be allotted to specific company-endorsed efforts or volunteer days. This allows the corporation to track overall volunteer time for the benefit of storytelling and quantifying community service hours and economic impact.

Tie employee engagement to corporate sponsorship. When a corporation pledges itself to community engagement, it commits its employees to this endeavor, as well, thus creating a symbiotic relationship. Employees are encouraged to become engaged in nonprofits and to donate their time, talents, energy – and, in some cases, their leadership on the nonprofit's committees or board. The corporation must serve as a support system for these volunteers; and one form of support is corporate sponsorship of events conducted by the nonprofits that are actively served by the company's employees. Corporations can set thresholds or designate sponsorship levels ahead of time based on different metrics; but the key is offering financial aid tied to the employee's service. Such funding shows support for both the nonprofits and the company's employees. The corporation, of course, benefits from the increased publicity and goodwill.

Tie corporate donations to volunteer hours. Tying corporate donations to volunteer hours is a wise strategy, particularly for two reasons. First, it enables the business to put a "face" on those corporate dollars, since the nonprofits benefiting from the financial support would be within the community. Equally important is the second reason: It adds "heart" to the donation because it ties the charitable giving to the very people who have physically engaged themselves in the community by investing their time, energy and talents to help the nonprofits. A bonus benefit, of course, is the personal recognition and encouragement – and the sense of pride – it affords the employees, whose efforts have "earned" the money for those nonprofits.

How a corporation chooses to "tie" the donation to volunteer hours is its choice; and the method can be designed in any number of ways. A basic plan, though, might be for the company to make a $500 donation to a nonprofit on behalf of an employee who has contributed 20 hours of his or her personal service to that organization. A company might also donate $100 for each employee who has worked on a given Saturday with a nonprofit. Companies could provide a matching fund program, too, so that if an employee personally contributed money to a cause, his or her donation automatically would be doubled, up to a pre-set amount. No matter how the money is donated, tying donations to volunteer hours makes this another win[3].

Aside from these three tactics to encourage employee volunteerism, companies can organize nonprofit tours and volunteer days; and also invite nonprofit leaders to speak at team meetings. We'll share some specific tips regarding coordinating nonprofit tours and volunteer days later in this chapter, but these experiential opportunities provide a unique and fun way for employees to learn more about the organizations making a difference in the community and to see the impact being made firsthand. These events foster teamwork and corporate pride, and help raise awareness for the nonprofit and its ongoing volunteer needs, as well.

Inviting a nonprofit leader to speak at a morning meeting or a hosted "Lunch & Learn" at the office is an easy way to fit an enrichment experience into a busy workday. Many nonprofit leaders can effectively present their organization's mission, programs, impact, and opportunities for support in as little as five to fifteen minutes, if necessary. Of course, offering more time, like over lunch, allows them to give a more in-depth overview and perspective. Either way, this format can be valuable if and when employees need to stay in the office.

For another easy way to engage employees without leaving the office, companies can adopt the "Casual Day." At Lipscomb & Pitts Insurance, we designate certain Fridays throughout the year as "Casual Fridays." Anyone who would like to dress in a more casual manner is asked to contribute at least $5, which goes to a selected charity that day. Each year, thousands of dollars are raised through these fun casual days and it's yet another simple way for our company to involve employees and show support for local charities. If your company already has a casual dress code, think of something else your employees would view as a perk and then ask them to make a donation in order to participate in that perk.

ADD ADVENTURE AND PURPOSE TO MEETINGS

Have you ever felt like your day is one endless meeting or you're having meetings to plan more meetings? If the answer is yes, then take special note of the following suggestions. With a little ingenuity and pre-planning, you can turn a routine meeting into an unforgettable adventure that can inspire your team to become more creative, productive employees; and your company, as a whole, to become more purpose driven and community engaged.

If your team fits in a car, SUV, or company van, do what we highlighted earlier and take your meeting on the road, delivering nutritious, hot meals to senior citizens with a program like MIFA's Meals on Wheels (mifa.org). Meet at your office in the morning, load up everyone in the vehicle, head to MIFA, pick up coolers packed with healthy lunches, and deliver the meals along a pre-determined route. This only takes about an hour and a half to complete. While on the road, the team can talk business; and, with each stop along the way, the conversation is likely to become increasingly energized and positive. The added benefit of this type of "road trip" comes from hand-delivering the meals and talking with the recipients, who are always deeply appreciative. Who wouldn't be uplifted by this fun and rewarding "work" session?

If you're planning a lunch meeting, team up with a nonprofit and host the lunch at its facility. Doing so would imbue yet another routine event with a new, refreshing atmosphere that sets the stage for giving back. For those living in the Memphis area, you could have the youth at JIFF (JIFFyouth.org) cook and serve the meal. This organization, located at 254 South Lauderdale Street in downtown Memphis, works with court-referred, adjudicated delinquent adolescents to equip them with the skills and support necessary to break the destructive cycle of criminal behavior. One of the organization's programs is a culinary school, where the youth learn how to prepare meals made from scratch and how to serve them. You'll enjoy a delicious lunch, accompanied by some thought-provoking dialog from the youth who share their personal stories of transformation. After the lunch meeting, take everyone on a quick tour of the facility so they can see firsthand how this transformation has taken place in the youth – and why personal engagement by members of the community, such as your attendees, could be truly life changing.

Instead of having your meeting indoors, take it outside and enjoy nature. Rent canoes and take a guided tour down a river, such as the Wolf River (wolfriver.org). Watch a herd of buffalo and have a picnic at a park like Shelby Farms Park (shelbyfarmspark.org). Brainstorm as you stroll through a garden like the Memphis Botanic Garden (memphisbotanicgarden.com). "Walk on the wild side" by going to a zoo, such as our famous Memphis Zoo (memphiszoo.org).

For high-adventure, go rock climbing or take your team to a challenge course. At Team BRIDGES, located in Memphis, team-building is developed while rock climbing and balancing 40 feet above the ground. The BRIDGES Challenge (a two-hour, customized experience led by the company's internationally trained staff) incorporates the AutoZone High Adventure Challenge Course and the Memphis Grizzlies Climbing Wall. An adventure like this will literally take your meeting to new heights!

If you prefer something less "physical," promote cultural arts by taking your team to a museum or art exhibit. The Dixon Gallery & Gardens (dixon.org) or Memphis Brooks Museum of Art (brooksmuseum.org) would be ideal.

Have one of their docents walk you through the exhibits and simply ask, "What do you see?" After people respond, then ask, "Why do you see that?" You'll be amazed by the conversations that ensue, by what you'll learn from (and about) your co-workers, and how much creative energy this experience generates. The true beauty in such an event is that you don't have to know anything about art. You can use the trip simply as an engagement tool to spark dialog and new ideas – and to strengthen the bond between team members.

If hugs and smiles brighten your day, start your meeting day with kids like those at a Porter-Leath Head Start Center (porterleath. org). The Center's team makes it easy and fun to play with the young children there. You can read, color, play dress up, and enjoy a beautiful day outside on the playground. The kids are full of life, love, and appreciation! This "play date" is easy to execute. Have your team meet at Porter-Leath, stay for 30 minutes, and then head out to your normal business meeting. Everyone will be super-charged with youthful enthusiasm and a much more positive attitude for subsequent business discussions. Thanks to a matching grant, too, the volunteer hours accrued by your team's interaction with the students will yield a financial contribution of about $15 per hour for Porter-Leath. Talk about a win[3]!

The key to breaking up the monotony of meetings is to intersperse these routine, ordinary functions with extraordinary opportunities for your team's personal and professional enrichment. The change of pace alone will invigorate employees and make them look forward to meetings. More importantly, the "learning and growing" aspect of each of these experiences will fully engage participants and help spark new and creative ideas, which will profit the company, the community, and the employees themselves. Although the examples I've offered are each tied to the Mid-South, you should easily be able to locate similar organizations and locales in your own area. The tactic of using meetings as conduits for exploring your city and sparking new ideas and opportunities for growth offers win[3] benefits that often exceed everyone's wildest expectations.

FOCUS ON THE TIME AND PEOPLE FOR SUCCESSFUL NONPROFIT TOURS & VOLUNTEER DAYS

Recently, I spoke to members of the Memphis Chapter of the American Marketing Association, which focuses on bringing together professionals in the field of marketing for career development, networking, and continuing education. At the conclusion of my presentation, a director of marketing for a local business asked for advice. She was trying to schedule nonprofit tours and was having difficulty getting buy-in from her team. The question she posed to me was, "How do I get them to participate?"

Many of us work for fast-paced, sales-driven organizations; and it can be a challenge to draw busy professionals out of the office to see the good taking place in our city. Without this motivation, though, how can employees be inspired for community engagement, even at a basic level? The two following tactics could be helpful.

TACTIC #1: Schedule volunteer opportunities or nonprofit tours at strategic times during the day, which are typically the start of the workday (8:30 AM), around lunch (Noon), or toward the end of the workday (3:30 PM). For nonprofit tours, it is usually best to schedule them either first thing in the morning (before people get to the office) or around lunch, which is a natural break. This is when most professionals like to schedule meetings, workshops, and other events. For a nonprofit tour, you should typically allot an hour, plus whatever drive time is needed.

When it comes to volunteer efforts, try to keep the events between one and two hours. If a longer timeframe is needed, create staggering opportunities or shifts that allow individuals to participate for short durations. With cityCURRENT, we usually set a flexible window of an hour and a half. We try to allocate 30 minutes for drive time, too. Using this plan, we'd encourage employees to leave work at 3:30 PM, so as to meet for after-school tutoring from 4:00 PM to 5:00 PM.

To track time volunteers are away from the office, you can allow those employees to modify their work schedules to compensate for the time they've been away; or you could simply consider their volunteer time as a part of your company's giving back efforts. Setting up multiple and consistent opportunities, either spread out over different days or at different times during a single day, enables employees to participate in shifts, thus covering for each other and preventing too many people being out of the office at the same time.

TACTIC #2: Prior to scheduling your tour or volunteer day, invite the nonprofit's Executive Director to attend a company meeting so he or she can personally connect with your employees and share with them an overview of the organization's activities and its purpose. It also could be advantageous to invite some of the nonprofit's board or committee members since it would expand interaction and increase the possibility that some of these people would know some of your employees and could, then, extend a personal invitation to those individuals to attend the tour or volunteer day. If it isn't possible to have anyone from the nonprofit come out to your office beforehand, don't worry. The real key is having the Executive Director and some of the nonprofit's board members confirmed to attend and lead your tour; and knowing their names in advance.

Once you've confirmed who'll be attending and leading the tour on behalf of the nonprofit, use that guest list to encourage your team, especially those in leadership and sales roles, to participate. Executives and sales representatives LOVE meeting business and community leaders because it broadens their network of contacts; so use this to your advantage and let them know in advance that they'll have the chance to meet and spend time with the Executive Director and board members. Add that it's an opportunity to interact with these leaders in a smaller, more intimate environment for at least an hour and that the context is community building and it should be easy to increase your attendance levels at these events. Also, being creative with how you publicize the event will help you attract the largest crowd possible. Having the head of your company in attendance, too, will send a clear message of support for the meeting and the tour.

STEP FOOT ON SCHOOL CAMPUSES

Attracting, developing, and retaining leaders and knowledge workers (i.e., professionals and experts whose main capital is knowledge, such as engineers, physicians, scientists, lawyers, accountants, and academics) is critical to sustaining a community's vitality. Ours is a world increasingly driven by technology; so knowledge workers and college-educated employees help set the stage for growth and development. Everyone wins when we can attract, develop, and retain valued workers by giving them opportunities to succeed. After all, today's ideas and visions are tomorrow's currency.

The significance of the preceding statement was made evident at a New Memphis Institute's Board of Governors meeting. A report showed that the economic impact of retaining around 800 knowledge workers in Memphis was estimated at over $54.5 million. That number indicated just the economic impact; it did not also factor in the social benefits derived from their civic engagement and leadership.

Here in the Mid-South, countless organizations, educational institutions, companies, and individuals are focusing on cultivating and retaining local talent. This effort, however, requires the support of the entire community, particularly our business leaders. Every one of us needs to be actively engaged with our students and young professionals, so these individuals know that their community wants them to stay and can provide the opportunities needed to make it possible.

Once you start looking around your hometown, you'll find a host of opportunities to work with teachers and other school personnel. Most schools, at all grade levels, host career days and expos, where entrepreneurs and professionals talk with students about different occupations and career opportunities. Throughout the year, they also offer special functions for interacting with students and sharing with them important stories and lessons learned. School systems often have debate teams, robotics teams, and other extra-curricular programs that provide community members unique opportunities for working with students, too.

There are endless opportunities to become more engaged with college students, as well. Interacting with college students can be mutually beneficial because you can build relationships with top talent and recruit these people to join your company after graduation. One of our local groups working to promote solid student-business relationships is the Leadership Education And Development program (LEAD) at the University of Memphis. The LEAD program is a holistic leadership platform that includes a four-year academic scholarship program, complete with classroom instruction, workshops, community projects, mentoring, and active engagement in campus and community organizations. Leadership with accountability is woven into every element of the student's on-campus and off-campus life. The program crosses all majors.

One component of the LEAD program that I'm heavily involved with is the Professional Connection Lunches. Our effort is to bring business leaders together with college students for fun, moderated conversations over lunch. We usually host three lunches per semester; and the events are held on the campus of the University of Memphis so students can easily attend after their morning classes. We group attendees in clusters of eight to ten people, half being students and half being professionals. We show a few short videos at the beginning to establish the theme, which ranges from personal branding to resumes, interviewing, and networking; and then we allow the groups to interact and share their feedback. It's an enlightening experience. Business leaders have the chance to share their expertise and wisdom; and the students can ask questions and also share their thoughts. These sessions produce valuable insight and allow the professionals and students to learn from each other.

If you live outside the Mid-South, reach out to your local college or university and consider replicating the Professional Connection Lunches. The model is simple, yet effective. It allows you the forum to engage students and business and community leaders in a brief, "snapshot mentoring" opportunity. Instead of a typical year-long, one-on-one mentoring relationship, this platform is an interactive, hour-and-a-half session, where viewpoints and advice are shared in a group setting, with no formal follow up or expectation beyond the event. If desired, you can distribute contact information for attendees or allow them to exchange business cards. Either way, this model makes it easy for everyone. Hosting such an event can help you connect with and develop future leaders; it can also give you a competitive advantage in attracting, developing, and retaining talent.

GIVING for GROWTH

A group of people often overlooked are the newcomers to a community. When new families move into town, it behooves us all to extend a welcoming hand to these fellow citizens and help them become rooted in our society. Many organizations here in Memphis routinely invite newcomers to receptions and dinners hosted at the homes of prominent business and community leaders with the intention of helping them form friendships. With every business contact made and friendship formed, members of these families can become more passionate about the city and more engaged in the community; but opportunities must exist to help and guide them. Some families, of course, will be transferred to other cities or have to move away for other reasons; but many families who are deeply ingrained in their community often pass up lucrative opportunities to move because they've made their current community home.

Strive, then, to step foot on school campuses and to open up your house to newcomers. Make your city or town a home to the very people who can make the community better, stronger, and more vibrant.

I hope you've found the tactics shared in this chapter to be helpful. Incorporate them into your own personal game plan for making your business a more successful partner in giving for growth. I also hope you'll encourage co-workers and other businesses in your community to join in this worthy effort so more positive outcomes can be achieved. Let's now turn our focus on nonprofits and examine proven tactics that can help strengthen and grow these organizations in your community.

THOUGHTS & ACTION STEPS

GIVING for GROWTH

Chapter Six

TACTICS FOR GROWTH: NONPROFIT

FUNDRAISING RELIES ON RELATIONSHIPS

Up to this point, we've primarily focused on volunteerism and the win[3] that it creates for individuals, businesses, and our community. I don't intend to lose this focus; but I want to shift gears momentarily and address the all-important concept of fundraising. Without adept fundraising, even the best nonprofits will struggle to operate effectively. Those that learn to raise money successfully will see their causes flourish. To most people, fundraising seems intimidating; but the reality is that each of us can be proficient at raising money because it fundamentally relies on relationships.

Fundraising is personal! On the surface, a corporation's monetary donation to a nonprofit appears impersonal; but behind each "gift" lies a personal storyline or a relationship that can be traced to someone in the company. It might be an employee, who is serving on the nonprofit's board; or it could be a request from a friend, vendor, client, or other civic leader. It might simply be a decision-maker's desire to help the effort. The bottom line, though, is fundraising is all about people helping people.

The hard part of fundraising is having to navigate the sea of competition with other worthwhile causes.

At Lipscomb & Pitts Insurance, we average about 13 requests per day for donations. All of these come from organizations doing amazing work; and many of the requests include elaborate presentations. Unfortunately, we simply cannot properly review, follow up with, and effectively build relationships with each group. Like everyone else, our company has to be selective, balancing the needs of nonprofits with our ability to give.

Once you understand these dynamics, you'll realize why this statement rings true: The shorter the "ask," the more money you can raise for a nonprofit you support. Who makes the "ask" is of utmost importance, though. In my experience, a short, personal note from a trusted friend, seeking the support, yields a much better return than any other solicitation.

For those of you taking your first steps in fundraising, I offer the following advice. Begin by reaching out to friends and family for small amounts; and encourage them to join you for a tour or a volunteer experience. This will result in larger donations down the road. If you serve on a nonprofit board, you need to plan your strategy carefully. As a board, ask yourself these questions: Who has the best relationship with a potential donor; or who should reach out to that person and start building a relationship for the future? This can truly become FUNdraising, once you realize that people enjoy helping and supporting their friends!

STACK THE DECK TO INCREASE SPONSORSHIP DOLLARS

My good friend, Michael Drake, Founder and CEO of masterIT, playfully compares his technology-as-a-service company to a Muddy's Bake Shop Prozac cupcake. Muddy's Bake Shop is a Memphis-based, independent bakery that has received national recognition for its cupcakes, cakes, cookies, pies, and other baked goods. Their Prozac cupcake is a chocolate cupcake with chocolate buttercream icing. (Side note: My younger son, Cayson, loves their cupcakes. If you're ever in Memphis, Muddy's is a "must do!") What Michael Drake says is this, "When you see the cupcake; when you smell it and take that first bite, it tastes amazing! You don't stop to think about all the individual ingredients, the chemistry that takes place in the oven or the careful effort put forth by the baker for it to taste like Heaven on earth; you're simply enjoying the cupcake. That's how it is with technology, too. You aren't focused on the infrastructure; you just need it to perform."

The same concept applies to events. Whether it's a concert, festival, corporate or nonprofit event, attendees just want to have fun and enjoy the experience. From that first step into the venue to the final applause – and everything in between – the true secret of success lies in the details.

An often overlooked, yet immensely important detail for increasing corporate sponsorships at fundraising events is personal introductions. Individuals who purchase tickets are typically supporters of the cause, friends or family of the host committee, or simply couples or families who want to enjoy a night of giving back. This group is excited about attending and has no heightened expectation for introductions.

Corporations, on the other hand, have much larger underwriting budgets; and they gauge event success much differently. I think all corporate sponsors of nonprofit events truly value the philanthropic purpose of such functions; but, as businesses, they have to take into consideration the ROI of those sponsorships. Even when Lipscomb & Pitts Insurance sponsors an event, we conduct an internal review to see if our brand was well represented and if our team was able to make business connections.

Hosts and nonprofits who recognize this dynamic can stack the deck in their favor. By holding a VIP reception prior to the event, they effectively create an ideal forum for sponsors, board members, and other influential supporters to congregate in a more intimate environment, one that is conducive for building new relationships and solidifying old ones. Hosts, who know some of these individuals, can serve as personal connectors. They can welcome guests and strategically introduce them to each other.

This purposeful action becomes a powerful tool for increasing sponsorships because the hosts can track and report the specific introductions made at the event back to the sponsoring company. This follow-up is extremely important because, in most cases, the people making the sponsorship decisions are not the same employees who attend the event. Hosts can optimize their efforts at the reception by researching, prior to the reception, commonalities between the guests in order to facilitate new relationships that can mutually benefit everyone.

WANT TO MEET MY BOARD?

People who are looking for a fun date night or something unique to do with family and friends can always find an upcoming nonprofit event, where they can have a great time and help others, too. The Mid-South's fundraising event calendar stays jam-packed year-round with fancy galas, festivals, 5K races, wine dinners, benefit concerts, golf scrambles, and more. These events provide valuable opportunities to raise awareness and much-needed funds for nonprofits; but the flood of functions competing for limited time and dollars presents a common challenge for the host organizations because each is striving to maximize its events' attendance and effectiveness.

A similar challenge arises in regard to securing corporate sponsorships for these events. As I mentioned earlier, we at Lipscomb & Pitts Insurance would like to accept every nonprofit's request for support of its worthwhile efforts; but this simply is not feasible. We must be selective in our choices – just like all businesses and families. If you're serving on a board or working with a nonprofit, though, don't be discouraged. I'll share with you two viable strategies you can utilize to leverage your board's power and increase sponsorships, ticket sales, and fundraising for any event.

The first is identifying "who knows whom best." At a scheduled meeting, determine each board member's sphere of influence and relationships with prospective supporters; and develop individual prospect lists, based on who has the strongest relationship with that supporter. Each board member, then, extends an invitation and makes the request of support to the people on his or her prospect list. A prospect is much more likely to attend an event or make a contribution when asked by a friend rather than an unfamiliar person!

The second is asking sponsors and potential sponsors whom they would like to meet at your event and then extending invitations to those preferred guests. Each sponsor purchases a table at the designated function; and then the nonprofit invites and furnishes a "free" pair of tickets to the prospects the sponsor has selected. The sponsor's guests would then be seated at his or her table. To woo prospective sponsors, show them a list of your current donors and board members; and ask if they would like an introduction to these community leaders.

The lesson to be learned here is that people are a powerful draw. Organizations that leverage their board and other relationships can expand their fundraising events to include strategic networking. This can attract new supporters and incentivize current supporters to increase their investment and attendance.

HELP ME, HELP YOU RAISE AWARENESS

Although fundraising is a main concern for virtually all nonprofit leaders, increasing awareness of their organization and recruiting volunteers for their endeavors present challenges of similar magnitude. People's personal and professional lives today are progressively growing busier! Consequently, nonprofits have to be even more innovative in their efforts to grab the public's attention, draw competent people into the fold, and cultivate these volunteers to be ambassadors for sustaining the organization's growth. A nonprofit's ability to be "turnkey," then, is its defining differentiator for success. The easier an organization makes it for people to give back, the easier it is to garner their support and employ their spheres of influence to help raise awareness for the group's charitable cause.

An excellent example of this is Ronald McDonald House Charities of Memphis. For each event the organization hosts, their leadership team develops a marketing plan that includes a "one-sheet," which is shared with board members and other volunteers. The one-sheet outlines the primary logistics; and, equally important, it details all the social media links, handles, #hashtags, and contact information for sponsors and partners. This one-sheet even provides options for verbiage that supporters can copy, paste, and post. By concisely compiling this information, the charity makes it effortless for volunteers to assist in creating a highly effective, free promotional blitz.

To make this strategy even more productive, I'd recommend creating and utilizing different URL shortened links – like using Bitly.com to track success among different groups and social media channels. Then, map out the timing, frequency, and preferred channels for your communications to ensure that volunteers are in sync on what, when, and where to post messages, along with what organizations or individuals to tag for maximum visibility and impact on social media.

At a time when everyone seems to have a smartphone and "selfies" are wildly popular, I find it quite interesting that most nonprofit event planners forget to designate a person or a team of people to handle social media and take pictures at their events. This is too important a detail to overlook! Many organizations will come up with a clever #hashtag for their event and promote it heavily before and during the event. Having a #hashtag allows you to not only market your organization, but also share and catalog the pictures and storylines both during and after the event.

Of additional value is having a videographer, who can interview participants and get plenty of action footage. This doesn't necessitate hiring a professional; any capable, creative person with a smartphone, notepad, and pen will do fine. The notepad and pen allow the videographer to jot down the names of individuals who were photographed or interviewed. This is important for sharing and tagging everyone in social media posts later. Capturing the storylines at your events and encouraging supporters to take their own pictures and video footage to share enables your organization to accumulate the needed resources for creating an impressive multi-media recap.

Having a recap with pictures and a short video, along with the notes of who participated, can be a huge advantage when it comes to marketing and publicity. It allows you to share and tag your social media posts effectively, so your chances of going viral increase. Make sure to share the recap with your organization, the companies that sponsored the event, and the people who helped with the cause! Posting pictures, videos, and blog entries that thank the sponsors and participants produces myriad benefits. Corporations and volunteers, of course, love the kudos and are more compelled to support future events. As participants share their pictures and experiences with family and friends, awareness of your cause is heightened; and the potential for attracting new volunteers and sponsors is exponentially increased, as well.

Each of the tactics I've just shared with you has a proven record of success with board members and nonprofit leaders. I've witnessed firsthand their effectiveness; and I'm always amazed by the win³ results each tactic produces. If you're currently involved with a nonprofit, share these strategies with your team, board members, and volunteers. Implement them for your next event; and see what positive effects they'll have on your efforts to increase public awareness and improve fundraising. If you're not currently involved with a nonprofit, take time today to find a local organization that mirrors your passions and needs your unique talents and skills. You'll have added value as a volunteer – and hopefully as a nonprofit leader, if you work for the organization – because of the insight and knowledge you've gained from reading this book.

Now let's proceed by sharing tactics for giving gifts that have purpose and give back.

GIVING for GROWTH

THOUGHTS & ACTION STEPS

GIVING for GROWTH

Chapter Seven

TACTICS FOR GROWTH: GIFT GIVING

One of my favorite quotes from Billy Graham, the famous Christian evangelist, is "God has given us two hands, one to receive with and the other to give with." The point he is making, of course, is that everyone has an intrinsic responsibility to help one another and that we must all give as much as we receive in life. This closely ties in with the Bible verse found in Luke 12:48: "From everyone who has been given much, much will be demanded; and from the one who has been entrusted with much, much more will be asked." Bill Gates, Co-Founder of Microsoft, the world's largest PC software company provided an even more concise version of this Bible verse, when asked by *Forbes* to share his advice for new college graduates: "From those to whom much is given, much is expected."

Anytime you are volunteering and working to make a difference in the lives of others, you are giving the gift of your time and talents. Anytime you donate to a nonprofit or contribute money to a worthy cause or a friend in need, you are giving a gift. Gifts come in all forms, shapes, and sizes. Some are tangible, such as money or clothing; others are intangible, such as mentoring a student or spending time with residents of a nursing home. The remarkable thing about giving a gift, though, is that the giver derives as much – or more – from this act of generosity than does the recipient. Anytime I talk with someone who has served as a mentor or taken part in a humanitarian trip, that person always comments that he or she received far more than they were ever able to give. Hence, the adage is true: It is better to give than to receive.

If you're a parent, as I am, you've most likely experienced that heart-warming feeling that comes from watching your children's joy in opening their birthday gifts or Christmas presents. That feeling is, in itself, a gift to us! Imagine the impact we could make if we applied the giving back mindset to all of our gift giving! It would be an incredible win[3]. To maximize your efforts in giving back, I hope you will implement some of the following tactics for giving gifts; and encourage your family, friends, and co-workers to do the same.

GIFTS THAT GIVE BACK

I love the spirit of cheerful giving that permeates the holiday season! Holidays make the perfect time to help people in need and to show love and appreciation to family, friends, fellow workers, teachers, and anyone else who is important in our lives. When it comes to gift giving, then, if you think "giving back," you'll "double the pleasure, double the fun" that each present provides.

Perhaps you need a gift for somebody who "has everything." Your present could be a donation to that person's favorite nonprofit. With LinkedIn and social media, it's easy to find the organizations people support because most list their board involvement on their profiles. Serving on a nonprofit board almost always carries the expectation of helping raise money; so making a contribution in honor of the board member will be deeply appreciated. It will also show that you care about the community and that you cared enough about the honored individual to learn what causes were important to him or her.

If you're a business owner, you can send clients and associates holiday cards that extend your company's good wishes for the season and let the recipients know that a charitable donation has been made on their behalf. This is what Pickering Firm, Inc., a Memphis-based engineering and architectural company, does each year. Pickering pre-selects the nonprofits; sends the firm's monetary contributions, in advance, to those organizations; then uses the holiday cards to inform the honorees of the donations in their name. Other companies take a slightly different approach by hosting an online version where each honoree is able to view a list of nonprofits and then select one as the recipient of the donation. Some companies go a step further and allow honorees unrestricted choices for the nonprofits. With either approach, these purpose-driven greeting cards raise funds and awareness for charities while spreading holiday cheer.

Another way of utilizing cards for giving back during the holidays is choosing those that support and promote nonprofits. Many organizations create custom cards for purchase and others will mail a handwritten, personalized holiday card on your behalf. Typically, the requested donation for these types of cards starts at $5 to $10. Sending custom cards or having a nonprofit mail a personalized card on your behalf means that your holiday cards will then be filled with joy and help raise awareness for the nonprofit, while also helping it give back to others.

As you shop for holiday gifts, purchase toys like colorful teddy bears, which can, in turn, be donated to a worthy cause on behalf of someone you know or love. One such worthy cause is the Memphis Child Advocacy Center (memphiscac.org). It's a nonprofit that helps children who are victims of abuse. As part of the healing process, each abused child who enters the program can select a teddy bear of his or her choice; so donating teddy bears in honor of friends, family, or co-workers helps comfort children as they endeavor to regain their trust in people.

If you enjoy shopping online, you'll find numerous philanthropic-oriented enterprises that offer exclusive products and services. Check out handmade jewelry at Same Sky (samesky.com), a group that helps create jobs for women in Sub-Saharan Africa. Their jewelry is worn by a host of celebrities; and the line includes colorful bracelets, ornate necklaces, and cufflinks. For the "health nuts" on your gift list, order food from NatureBox (naturebox. com). They will enjoy receiving delicious, healthy snacks each month; and for each gift box delivered, the company donates one meal through Feeding America.

Visit City Dining Cards (citydiningcards.com) if you need a useful stocking stuffer. The site offers a deck of discount cards for $20. Each deck contains fifty $10 discount cards to locally owned restaurants. For each $20 purchase, $11 is donated by the company to local charities. As recipients use the discount cards, they'll be adding extra value to your gift because their support of local business owners and artisans is helping these people give back to others, as well.

T-shirts make great gifts, too, especially when proceeds of these sales help fund giving back efforts. If you live in the Mid-South or want to show your love of Memphis, I encourage you to purchase "Memphis Rocks" shirts. "Memphis Rocks" is a civic pride campaign that was launched in 2012 to promote Memphis and support the Fallen Officer Memorial, which is a one million-dollar, 100 percent privately-funded project honoring the Memphis Police Department and Shelby County Sheriff's Office Officers who have lost their lives in the line of duty. The shirts come in different colors and designs, short and long sleeves. The original edition, which we helped to create, features a listing of many iconic landmarks, organizations, and people who make our community special, in the shape of a music note.

Clothing companies like Memphis-based Agape North (agapenorth.com) follow a one-for-one model and operate much like a nonprofit. For each shirt Agape North sells, it donates a school uniform to a student in need. The company offers a wide variety of polo shirts, t-shirts, caps, scarves, and outerwear. Businesses can order in bulk and customize some of their designs; and they can work with Agape North to select nonprofit beneficiaries in their own cities.

Another outlet for "T-shirts for a cause" is tshirtchampions.com. The website is owned by cityCURRENT partner, Champion Awards & Apparel, which is one of the largest T-shirt printers in the country. You can work with the Champion team from anywhere in the world to design your shirts – like we did with our "Memphis Rocks" T-shirts – and then set up a program through which proceeds can benefit a nonprofit of your choice. T-shirt and clothing sales can be powerful marketing tools for raising awareness and funds. To learn just how far-reaching this marketing strategy can be, read the following story about Patrick Otema.

PATRICK SPEAKS

On November 12, 2014, Lipscomb & Pitts received a phone call from a reporter asking for information regarding our involvement with deaf children in Uganda. Although we support mission trips to all parts of the world to rehabilitate homes and schools and we work with organizations that have outreach in Uganda, we were unaware of any mission trip fitting the reporter's description. Consequently, he shared with us "Patrick Speaks," a video uploaded to YouTube by Channel 4 in the United Kingdom.

The video featured Patrick Otema, a 15-year old who was born deaf and was living in a remote part of Uganda. Patrick had never before had a conversation; but, in this powerful video, we were able to witness the transformation in Patrick's life, as he learned to speak for the first time through sign language. Over 1.6 million viewers had already watched this video.

Interestingly, the connection between Patrick's story, Memphis, and our company was that, in the video, Patrick is wearing a Lipscomb & Pitts T-shirt. What a surprise this was for us! We contacted the producer of the video, Daniel Bogado, through social media; and he, in turn, connected us with SignHealth, the U.K.-based charity working with Patrick and his teacher, Raymond Okkelo. Lipscomb & Pitts has joined SignHealth's support team, so we can truly be part of Patrick's story and the stories of others like him in Uganda.

We may never know how Patrick got that shirt. (My mother, however, steadfastly believes that it was given to Patrick as part of a shoebox gift for "Operation Christmas Child," the well-known project of Samaritans' Purse, the relief organization led by Rev. Franklin Graham.) Regardless of how Patrick ended up with our shirt, we're pleased he's gotten good use from it; and we hope he's still "feeling the love" from Memphis and from all of us at Lipscomb & Pitts. Patrick's story serves as a powerful reminder that geography does not limit our ability to make a difference and that giving gifts can have far-reaching, life-changing effects!

GIVING for GROWTH

SECRET SANTA 2.0

The holiday season is a great time for everyone to enjoy corporate festivities and to show appreciation to dedicated employees and loyal clients. If you're noticing a lack-luster response to long-standing traditions like Secret Santa, however, an "upgrade" to that tradition is now available and can be readily installed in your family or business operations. I think you'll like this upgrade!

For decades the employees of Lipscomb & Pitts Insurance participated in the surprise gift-giving game of Secret Santa. In keeping with the game's guidelines, each employee acted both as a Secret Santa, who gave a gift to a co-worker, and as a recipient of a gift given by a different Secret Santa. An individual would first draw the name of a co-worker, then, consult a pre-made spreadsheet that showed the "drawn" person's preference of a gift, which usually was a gift card. The price limit for Santa's gift was not to exceed $10.

Personally, I liked the idea of showing appreciation and building camaraderie among the team; but when a mass email asking employees to cast a "for" or "against" vote for continuing the tradition was received, I began thinking it was time for a change. With everyone so busy and with nonprofits and our community in need of support, perhaps we could devise a new, more productive model for holiday giving. Thus, Secret Santa 2.0 was born.

Secret Santa 2.0 uses the same gift level of $10 per employee, but combines all the gifts into one, so as to achieve much greater good. Instead of the employees swapping individual gift cards, then, their cash contributions are pooled; and the group decides which one or more nonprofits are to receive the monetary gift. This model, could be easily modified to allow employees to purchase actual gifts like toys or teddy bears, which can be donated to a specific nonprofit (or a seasonal project like Toys for Tots). The company might also opt to invite the nonprofit to its annual holiday party or host a celebration event together with the nonprofit.

Secret Santa 2.0 is an upgraded model that engages employees to give back. It also impacts our community by leveraging collected resources. It cultivates philanthropy and teamwork because the employees select the nonprofit(s); and it raises awareness of and provides funds to local charities. I'm proud that our Lipscomb & Pitts Insurance team has now adopted a version of this upgraded Secret Santa 2.0 and has employed it with great success. I encourage you to make a similar transition.

THERE IS ALWAYS TIME FOR A BOOK

We often hear the saying, life isn't a destination; it's a journey. That journey, however, is filled with ups and downs, setbacks and successes, heartaches and love; yet each leg of the trip holds the potential of enriching our lives when we connect and communicate with our fellow travelers. Sharing life experiences through stories creates bonds that allow us to help others, accomplish our personal goals, and create legacies. Life is, indeed, a journey! It's also a story we each are writing and sharing every day!

Stories come in all forms. Even when we live in such a fast-paced society and our time is typically in short supply, most of us make time to enjoy a book. Books bring parents and children together for developing reading skills and fostering imagination. Books also encourage intellectual growth and provide the reader with a wealth of knowledge that can literally be the difference between poverty and success, isolation and integration. While there is nothing wrong with utilizing social media, there is a big disparity in learning derived from reading a text and reading texts.

For this reason, books will always be valuable gifts; and these gifts can become treasures when the books have a higher purpose. Such books help raise community awareness; and proceeds from their sales benefit worthwhile nonprofits. When you purchase a book from a locally-owned bookstore, you initiate the trifecta of giving a gift that enriches the recipient, impacts local jobs and commerce, and enables charitable organizations to continue helping others in the community.

If you live in the Mid-South and want a fun book to read, purchase a copy of *Feeding Memphis: A Celebration of the City's Eclectic Cuisine*. It features 28 locally owned restaurants and provides backstories, photographs, and favorite recipes; so you can cook your way through the book! With each copy sold, $10 is donated to the Mid-South Food Bank. If you prefer a gripping story, though, buy *Writing Our Way Home: A Group Journey Out of Homelessness*. The book, written by 15 individuals who overcame homelessness with help from Door of Hope (www.doorofhope. org), shares both the personal stories of the authors and the harsh realities of homelessness. It also offers advice on combating this societal problem and provides the reader with updates on where the authors are today.

I'd be remiss not mentioning that this book and my first book, *Giving Back with Purpose*, make great gifts, too. One hundred percent of the proceeds from each book gives back by supporting youth literacy programs in the Mid-South. Thanks to readers like you, we've been able to raise and contribute thousands of dollars to nonprofits focused on improving the literacy rates of children here in the Memphis area. By simply purchasing this book, you have helped us support these efforts; and for your help I am truly grateful. After reading this book, I hope you'll be compelled to buy additional copies as gifts for your friends, family, or co-workers. More importantly, I hope you'll become an advocate for purposeful gift giving and serve as an example for others to emulate.

Before moving on to a new topic, I want to offer a few final comments on some of the ideas I've shared earlier in this chapter. Just because you don't have a Memphis Child Advocacy Center in your area, rest assured you can find local or nearby nonprofits that offer – both around the holidays and throughout the year – creative gift-giving opportunities that will support them and help others. With some imagination and collaboration with others, you can transform holiday traditions and life celebrations into giving back events that can move everyone one step closer to the true meaning of giving. I've seen some amazing, creative gifts from family, friends, and colleagues; and I'd enjoy and appreciate hearing about your giving back gift stories, as well!

Let's "wrap" up this section and now look at tactics for personal growth that you can utilize in your journey toward achieving success. You can enjoy a rewarding life, while, at the same time, make a positive impact on the lives of others.

THOUGHTS & ACTION STEPS

GIVING for GROWTH

Chapter Eight

TACTICS FOR GROWTH: PERSONAL

I've said it before and I'll say it once again: Giving back is ALWAYS the right thing to do! As you've seen throughout this book, giving back is also fundamental to growth in your personal and professional life. Volunteering with nonprofits and community efforts provides prime opportunities to showcase your leadership skills, while meeting new people and expanding your sphere of influence. Civic engagement also gives you a point of differentiation from your peers and common ground when conversing with executives.

Business leaders are engaged in nonprofits and community development projects because they understand the importance of servant leadership and the symbiotic relationship between a vibrant city and a successful company. They astutely realize that the more they give to help improve the quality of life for the citizens in their community, the more potential benefits they will receive. Giving back, though, means leaders personally contribute financially and strategically to their community. They offer their time and expertise to make a difference.

If you're at a point in your career where you're content, it's easy to align your passions and expertise with organizations that have like needs. If you're looking for a job or want to make a change, though, you can create progress by working backward. Make a list of the companies you might like to work for and people you want to meet; then research online to learn what nonprofits they support. Between LinkedIn and Google, it's easy to find plenty of helpful information.

Once you've made note of the boards your selected business leaders serve on, start by reaching out to one or two of those nonprofits and offer to help with an upcoming event or initiative. Choose something manageable, with a short timeframe, and where you can take a leadership role that plays to your strengths (thus ensuring excellence in execution). Your only request should be that the nonprofit furnish you a written testimonial or, better yet, email a thank you to their board (and cc you).

Even if you're not able to meet the desired business leader in the process of volunteering, you can still benefit from the experience. The emailed thank you to the board will afford you the necessary platform to follow up with the desired person. In essence, the thank you becomes the key for opening up dialog between you and the business leader or perhaps even locking in an interview. Establishing a common ground of interest is definitely a smart tactic! You, of course, would mention that you enjoyed helping the nonprofit; and you might extend an offer to help with another of the nonprofit's undertakings, especially one that might be more of a personal goal for the business leader. The responsibility would rest on your shoulders, though, to make good on this offer; but a genuine offer of help can certainly pave the way for building a REALationship. Many of my friends have followed this exact process and landed dream jobs; so the tactic CAN work!

CREATE THE POSITION YOU WANT

Today's super-connected world affords people easy access to myriad people, information, and opportunities. Individuals who are willing to commit their time and efforts to personal growth can successfully develop new skillsets, such as learning to use graphic arts programs, like Adobe Photoshop and Illustrator. These new skillsets can increase a person's corporate value; but more importantly, they can enable the individual to take full control of his or her personal brand, build a powerful sphere of influence, and take command of his or her destiny. All of this takes time to build, though. The challenge is that most companies are sales-driven and expect instant results. They typically are faced with having to do more with less, too. Corporate engagement rarely has an immediate or easily measured outcome. So, it takes someone with vision, creativity, passion, and patience to turn giving back into a full-time job.

If you have the heart of a servant leader or you want to change the course of your career, take the initiative to volunteer. Companies like to be linked with positive news and outcomes; and they typically take note of their employee's volunteer achievements. Showing that can you successfully plan and execute a nonprofit's project or event can prove a valuable asset for you, particularly if you're seeking to make a lateral or upward move in your company. Community service achievements often work in your favor if you are job hunting, too, since they can give you that all-important edge over your competition. You should keep in mind, though, that building the foundation for success begins with your own personal efforts – and on your own time; it may take a while for people to notice your success and offer you a full-time opportunity.

This tactic can produce the results you desire. I have many friends who took it upon themselves to create give back and volunteer-led programs with their companies. They did a great job and built such successful programs that they now lead community relations efforts at their respective firms. By taking a similar initiative and realizing that it is within your power to create the position you want, your potential for success is truly limitless!

TWO TIPS FOR STANDING OUT FROM THE CROWD

If you want to stand out and be "memorable," you have to do things **DiFfErEnTlY**. In marketing terms this is called differentiation; and it encompasses the total experience we create when we interact with each other. This includes how we shake hands; how we make, or avoid, eye contact with others; the clothes we wear; the stories we share; the things we post on social media; the company we keep; and the type of energy we exude. It is being "authentic," yet confident enough to add flair.

When it comes to networking, your ability to stand out rests on something fundamental: preparation! People who are the most successful reach out to event coordinators ahead of time, asking for the names of the individuals who will be attending. They browse social media to find out who is promoting and sponsoring the event. They search LinkedIn and Google for pictures and profile information that includes community engagement. Nowadays, it's easy to find the boards that leaders serve on, the organizations they support, and their interests.

When you walk into the room, be prepared! Know people's names and faces, and the things that interest each of them. Avoid beginning your conversation with the generic "What do you do?" Opt for the more dramatic entrance, "Aren't you on the board of that great community nonprofit, [nonprofit's name]?" People will notice the difference; and even after the event is over, they'll remember that your conversation focused on community engagement.

Take differentiation a step further with your wardrobe. For example, I always try to wear something that will grab people's attention; it may be colorful shoes, a paperclip tie bar, or an array of eye-catching bracelets that support a cause, like women working in Africa or finding a cure for cancer. I make sure to not overdo it, but always have one "statement" piece that is sure to stand out. Doing something similar can be a fun way to show off your unique personality; it can also serve as an interesting icebreaker for conversation, particularly when the item you're wearing supports a charitable cause or has a personal storyline associated.

Do your research prior to attending an event and wear one purposeful item that serves to pique interest; you'll be surprised by how much you'll stand out from the crowd!

ADVICE FROM THE MULYP EMPOWERMENT CONFERENCE

Each year the Memphis Urban League Young Professionals (MULYP) hosts an Annual Empowerment Conference. Hundreds of young professionals from around the nation come to our city for a two-day event, which is packed with guest speakers, workshops, panel discussions, business expos, and social events. The topics range from personal branding to "Redefining Philanthropy" and "Work Life Balance – Does it Exist?" With its sellout crowd, the event is a huge success in helping equip and unite young leaders, as well as in marketing Memphis.

At last year's conference, I had the privilege of moderating the "Enhance Your Career Through Volunteering" workshop, which included a panel of four national experts. Among the helpful advice offered by that panel were three tidbits I want to share as a follow-up.

First, create a one-sheet with pictures and logos of your affiliations – i.e. nonprofits you support and schools you attended – to display outside your office. This advice was offered by Brandi Richard, President of the National Urban League Young Professionals. She explained that this gives guests and co-workers a chance to get to know her better. It serves as an ice-breaker and makes it easier to connect with people, while promoting the nonprofits she supports.

Second, make your employer aware of your volunteer efforts and the nonprofits you support. Employers appreciate knowing this information, especially if their employees are serving on boards or committees. This makes them aware of the responsibilities and enables them to connect the dots with those valuable relationships. Most companies will subsequently find ways to support the nonprofits that their employees are helping. To increase this type of volunteer awareness, Carlos Clanton, Executive Director of the Norfolk Education Foundation, recommended that nonprofits send welcome letters to the employers of their new volunteers, thanking those volunteers for their engagement and highlighting those people's efforts.

Third, understand that you are a champion for the nonprofit. One of the most pressing needs of an organization is raising awareness; so you can utilize social media and relationships to highlight the good being done at the nonprofit and how much fun you are having volunteering there. This can inspire others to become involved, too. Once you view yourself as a champion for your cause and start celebrating its efforts and successes, you'll find your excitement becomes contagious and your impact becomes greater!

ADVICE TO YOUNG PROFESSIONALS

Some time ago, I had lunch with a talented young professional who is forging his path here in our community. He grew up in Memphis, graduated from the University of Memphis, and now works at ServiceMaster. I knew of him through social media and his engagement in the community; so when he reached out through Twitter to set up our meeting, I was pleased to have the opportunity to connect with him in person; and I accepted his invitation.

Taylor Oaks serves as a great example of what business leaders discuss regarding talent development and retention. After graduation, he chose to start his family in Memphis and decided to make a difference here. I'm confident that Taylor's positive attitude and desire to grow will enable him to thrive as he continues to learn, absorb new ideas, and meet more leaders, who will help further shape his perspectives and future. Taylor is working hard; and he's willing to step out of his comfort zone, reaching out to unfamiliar leaders in order to achieve success.

If you are a young professional, too, it's important that you likewise understand that the world holds great promise for success, but that you must be the driving force for reaching your potential and realizing your dreams. Remember that all your opportunities in life will come from people; fulfilling your destiny necessitates your maintaining a positive attitude and a willingness to be proactive. Ignore naysayers! The sooner you acknowledge that you are the sole controller of your outlook and your responses, the faster you can rise to the top.

Memphis is ripe with global opportunities; yet it's intimate enough to connect with almost anyone. Ours is definitely a handshake – and relationship-driven city! Community engagement and helping others is vital for your credibility. Identify those leaders you want to meet and reach out to them by sharing coffee or lunch. Approach the meeting with a selfless attitude and a genuine desire to learn. If you want to make a great – and lasting – first impression, ask the leader to tell you one way he or she is involved in the community and one way you can help that organization or project. Successfully fulfilling a commitment to help can certainly open doors of opportunity for you in no time!

WHAT ARE YOU DOING FROM 5:30 PM TO 8:30 AM?

Recently, I caught up with a young professional who I've been mentoring for about three years. We talked about opportunities and challenges he was facing both at work and in his personal life and relationships. Most of the conversation focused on growth, though, and how he could be more intentional to develop his skills and sphere of influence, as well as increase his likelihood for a promotion.

The good news is that those three things are interconnected – developing your skills and sphere of influence increases opportunities for career advancement. However, there is no substitute for hard work and you must develop those skills and build those relationships, both inside the office and outside in the community, on your own time. My friend, Roscoe Bufkin, Vice President of Marketing Communications for Mueller Industries, Inc., based here in Memphis, puts it like this: "Performance and productivity are EXPECTED from 8:30 AM to 5:30 PM; promotions are EARNED as a result of what you do from 5:30 PM to 8:30 AM." Indeed, Roscoe is right!

As an employee, you are entrusted to fulfill the duties of your job description in the most expert and professional manner. It's similar to parents expecting their child to have near perfect attendance at school and always doing his or her best on classwork, homework, and tests, in order to receive an "A." We live and work in a highly-competitive, globally-connected environment where an "A" is the basic benchmark, though; not the differentiator. Differentiators are the extra-curricular activities – the things he or she does outside of the classroom, like sports, student government, debate, and volunteerism. It's what you highlight on a college application; and it's the same in business! What's the EXTRA that makes you a leader, unique, and valuable?

As we've discussed throughout this book, corporations strive to hire leaders, who will represent them well inside and outside the office. They're looking for people who will take initiative to learn new skills and get engaged in the community. Your new skills foster innovation and higher productivity levels; your engagement builds relationships and goodwill in the community that also benefit the company. So, if you really want to earn a promotion, use 5:30 PM to 8:30 AM to your advantage!

ADVICE TO GRADUATES

Last May, my home church held a baccalaureate service, recognizing the year's high school and college graduates who are members of our congregation. During the service, they played a slide show that featured each graduate maturing from a toddler to an adult. The show was synchronized with a live performance from Marc Lewis, who sang his song, "Goodbye (The Graduation Song)." There wasn't a dry eye in the house! The moment was an emotional reminder that May is both an exciting time of new beginnings and a bittersweet end to days past. Graduations and celebrations are held to honor achievement; but these events cause us to reflect on the past and realize how quickly our children have grown.

With graduation in mind, I'll share three pieces of advice that I wish I'd taken to heart sooner in life. First, believe that everything happens for a reason. While we encourage kindness, respect, and helping others, the reality is that the world is not always kind. More often than you would like, people and situations in life challenge your will and can leave you broken, bitter, or in tears. Realizing that these setbacks are "opportunities for growth," however, empowers you to become stronger and wiser, more patient and persistent. You can then view negative experiences as opportunities to strengthen your resolve to be a positive influence – on yourself and others. The greatest challenges hold the potential of yielding the greatest returns. (Remember, how you choose to respond to any given situation impacts your destiny.) The people I admire most didn't get to the top because everything went smoothly for them; they got there because when things went wrong, they chose to persevere!

Second, dare to explore and try something new. Travel and learn about other cities, countries, cultures, languages, and values. By learning from others, you'll learn more about yourself – and make lifelong friends in the process. Different perspectives lead to new ideas! Try new foods, take a challenging class, volunteer at different nonprofits, or strike up a conversation with a stranger. Curiosity doesn't "kill the cat;" it opens new doors, presents opportunities, and creates amazing stories for you to share.

Third, remember that everyone has value. We've all made and will continue to make mistakes. We can be loving and sweet most times, yet highly annoying other times. When we strive daily to treat everyone with kindness, respect, and love, however, we create a positive environment, which sets the stage for good things to happen – particularly when you're helping others.

JOINING NONPROFIT BOARDS: DON'T WAIT TO BE ASKED

Joining the board of a nonprofit can be an immensely rewarding and valuable way to give back and make a positive impact on your city. Board engagement affords the opportunity to help shape the vision and strategy for an organization, to ensure that it stays true to its mission, and to garner sufficient support for the nonprofit's effective and efficient operation. These are powerful mechanisms for professional and personal growth! Ask this fundamental question, "What does the community need us to do?" Then, diligently work to help the board find effective ways for bringing the answer to life.

All nonprofits are required to have a board of directors. According to a recent board training presentation by Mark Dean, former Executive Director of Volunteer Mid-South (now known as Volunteer Memphis), there are more than 2 million open board seats across the nation; and most nonprofits will have at least three vacancies each year. Consequently, there's a tremendous, continuous need for service.

Due to various factors, most nonprofits tend to go through the same referral networks to seek new board members. Chances are that the leadership of a board that would be the perfect fit for you doesn't know you exist; and, if they do, they might not be aware of your interest to serve. Nonprofits are always seeking new advocates, new ideas, and increased diversity. So, instead of waiting to be invited, take it upon yourself to start exploring organizations that align with your passions. By doing some research, you can determine which of the nonprofit functions, special events, or tours will best serve your needs for making known your interest in joining the board.

Be mindful, though, that boards have important legal and fiduciary responsibilities that necessitate a commitment of time, skills, and resources. Many board decisions require a quorum, too, so regular attendance by members is critical. Although expectations vary with nonprofits, almost all groups maintain some presumption of a financial contribution to the organization by members of the board. This is because anytime a nonprofit completes a grant request or asks for funding, it is asked about the percentage of board support. It makes a big difference when the organization can state "100 percent!"

Online research can yield you a number of great resources that provide information and questions to ask prior to joining a board. We've further facilitated this process for people here in the Mid-South by partnering with The Assisi Foundation of Memphis, Inc. to host an ongoing series of "Get On Board" nonprofit board workshops that cover topics ranging from "Board Service 101" to tips on fundraising and how to review financial statements. These lunch events are free and open to the public; so if you live or work in the Mid-South, check out cityCURRENT.com for upcoming events. You can also download a free PDF covering the things to consider and questions to ask prior to joining a board from our website. This valuable information can prove helpful in your selection process.

BENEFICIAL WATCH PARTY

A "beneficial watch party" is a time-tested favorite when it comes to weaving giving back into your everyday life. Almost every weekend presents a prime opportunity to have fun watching your favorite games, while easily and effectively raising money and awareness for a nonprofit you support.

The plan is simple: host a watch party at your house and invite your family and friends, telling them in advance that the event will benefit your selected nonprofit. As host, you provide the normal food and drinks; but ask attendees to consider donating to your nonprofit the amount of money they would typically spend for lunch or dinner. You'll be pleasantly surprised how much money one of these events can raise. Whether your team wins or loses, your event will always enjoy the true victory – helping other people.

Watch parties are perfect for football and basketball games, many types of television shows or awards shows – even a movie night at your house. You can apply this same concept to a birthday party, backyard cookout, or swim party. If you're a golfer or avid game player, you can try a variation and encourage your friends to play a nonprofit round or two. In this scenario, you could take a collection of $10 or $20 per mulligan and the winning player or team then is able to give all of the money to their favorite charity. Either way, beneficial watch parties are flexible functions that work well with people of all ages.

I've heard great success stories about families and college students equally raising hundreds and even thousands of dollars by hosting these types of events. In fact, one friend who accepted a challenge of hosting a "beneficial watch party" raised $15,000 during the course of a NFL season! He invited friends over each Sunday to watch the games; and what started as $25-dollar donations soon became $50-contributions, as the participants started becoming competitive and "bought" into the idea of helping others while watching the games. Then, about halfway through the season, his family and friends had become so impressed by what he was doing and by the impact it was having on the nonprofit, they started hosting their own "beneficial watch parties" to help, as well. So, not only was my friend able to raise a large amount of money to help his nonprofit, he was able to inspire many others to become philanthropists, as well! For this next football season, my friend is thinking about adding college football into the mix and raising the goal to more than $20,000!

Raising money for a nonprofit is an important contribution, but so is raising the public's awareness of that organization. If you host a "beneficial watch party," have on hand literature about the nonprofit, encourage the attendees to visit the group's website, and share your personal stories about your work at the organization or a testimonial about why you selected the nonprofit. By doing these things, just as my friend did above, you are serving as a role model and encouraging the people in your sphere of influence to join you in making giving back an integral part of everyday life.

FINDING YOUR VOICE

I had the pleasure of moderating a panel discussion at the 2014 Mid-South Book Festival. The conversation focused on "How to get your book published," which is a goal of most writers. With so many online resources and self-publishing options, it has never been easier to publish a book; however, for these same reasons, it is becoming harder for a writer to find his or her voice and to build an audience.

Much like singer/songwriters participating in open mic nights or bands distributing demos to win over fans, writers must find opportunities to connect with readers and build a following in order for their books to be successful. This dynamic sets the stage for nonprofits, businesses, and city leaders to utilize the talents of aspiring authors and creative professionals, who can start blogs or submit content that offers insight and uplifts the community, in return for literary exposure.

I use as an example the cityCURRENT blog, River City Rising. Launched in 2014, the blog is authored by Cherita Jackson, or "CJ" Kirkland, as we know her. CJ is a talented writer, who enjoys sharing the heartfelt stories of everyday heroes. She was born in the Bahamas and has lived in other U.S. cities like New York and Los Angeles (where she met her husband, Andre). When CJ and I first met, she mentioned she was looking for an avenue to use her gifts in a way that would inspire others, while opening new eyes to her work. Thus, the River City Rising blog became that conduit. It has been a wonderful addition to cityCURRENT; and our partnership with CJ has provided a fresh perspective on the Mid-South.

If you enjoy writing, explore possibilities for teaming up with a nonprofit or organization where you can showcase and hone your craft, while developing your fan base. You may start off doing this, as a passion, for free; but the pay-off will come, in time, if you brand that passion with your name and social contact information. You will find your voice once people find you.

As former publishing executive turned bestselling author Michael Hyatt has stated, there are three voices you can write from: 1) The Expert, who has been there and done it many times; 2) The Sherpa, who is not an expert, but has navigated the mountain before and can help guide you; or 3) The Journeyman, who is honest in sharing his or her experiences along the way. Once you find your voice and grow your audience, you can begin to leverage your influence for good!

JUST SHOW UP

Making a difference in the lives of others does not have to cost a cent. I'm reminded of this each January, when cityCURRENT teams with the Memphis Grizzlies and the Memphis Grizzlies Foundation to host our annual MLK National Day of Service - Samaritan's Feet Shoe Distribution. Each year, this event becomes larger. Last year, the service day brought together hundreds of volunteers – including Memphis Grizzlies' players Mike Conley, Jr. and Tony Allen, and former NBA player, Jason Collins – to wash the feet of more than 250 local youth and provide each of these youngsters with new shoes, socks, and a lot of love.

Our partnership with Samaritan's Feet began in 2010, when we had the organization's founder, Emmanuel "Manny" Ohonme, speak at our cityCURRENT Signature Breakfast. Manny grew up in Lagos, Nigeria; and when he was nine years old, his life was forever changed. A missionary from Wisconsin invited him to enter a contest for which the prize was a pair of shoes. The chance to own his first pair of shoes was too tempting to ignore.

As you probably expected, Manny won the contest and the prized new pair of shoes; but that prize held for the boy more gifts than he could ever have imagined. The missionary helped Manny learn to play basketball; and those shoes ultimately helped him earn a college scholarship and an education here in the United States. The missionary also encouraged Manny to believe in his dreams – to reach for the sky and never doubt he could touch the stars! Today, Manny is truly living out his dreams. Together with his wife and family, he is working passionately to change the lives of kids around the world and to be a solution for the 1.5 billion people worldwide who currently face foot-born infection and diseases and the one million children who die each year from those diseases.

Samaritan's Feet (samaritansfeet.org) was formed, in 2003, with the goal of giving 10 million children new shoes; and the organization is well on its way to reaching that goal. As of January 2015, over 6.5 million children have been "sole" blessed. The shoe distribution events, however, transcend new shoes and socks. They focus on the compassion of adults serving our youth by washing their feet, bonding through stories and laughter, and understanding that even a single act of kindness can have a BIG impact on a child's future.

As I walked around the event this year, thanking volunteers, I was surprised to learn that some of them had no prior affiliation with any of the host companies. They simply had seen the event online or on social media and shown up without any prior knowledge or expectations of the event. I received so much gratitude from the volunteers that I was completely overwhelmed. THEY were the ones who were serving the kids in Memphis; and, yet, they were thanking ME for the experience. So, who was the giver; and who was the receiver of this giving back gesture?

A comment that Mike Bowen, President of Champion Awards and Apparel, made to me that day reaffirmed something I already knew: "Ninety percent of success is just showing up!" Mike is correct. By each person taking the time and making the effort to show up at our event, we were able to achieve remarkable success. We formed new friendships, created treasured memories, and enriched the lives of everyone. You may not be in a position to host a Samaritan's Feet Shoe Distribution; but you can give back to children in other forms of volunteering, such as helping children learn to read, coaching after-school sports, or serving as a tutor or mentor.

A RESOLUTION TO DO LESS

Mark Cuban is best known as the billionaire owner of the Dallas Mavericks; but he is also one of the investors on the television series, *Shark Tank*. Because of his business acumen, Mark is often quoted. One such quote, which I recently saw on Facebook, is: "Work like there is someone working 24 hours a day to take it away from you." Since I grew up playing competitive tennis, I spent most of my youth leaving everything on the court, be it during drills or grinding it out in a match. Whatever I may have lacked in natural ability, I more than made up for in training harder and more effectively than others to become more technically sound and physically fit than my competitors. This discipline and hard work paid off for me in wins, rankings, and even a career.

Developing the mentality to push yourself beyond perceived limitations and the standard call of duty helps you achieve success in life and business. With this higher level of commitment, your determination radiates and becomes contagious, which opens more new opportunities. Hard work, perseverance, and dedication are all admirable qualities; but in today's world, where work and life are so fully integrated (i.e. our phones, laptops, and social media), we need to be careful not to overwork ourselves. We need to find a healthy balance. For me, this is a daily challenge.

The same competitive mentality that created my prowess on the tennis court can, in turn, have a counterproductive influence on my personal life. If I'm not careful to keep this in check, I stand to lose out on sharing precious moments of happiness with my wife and children. I don't want this to happen! I've heard far too many executives express regret for focusing so intensely on business that they missed priceless time with family. Their well-intended thought was work hard today for tomorrow's comfort. Tomorrow becomes today, though; if we don't "stop and smell the roses," we'll miss out on those opportunities for creating precious memories.

Giving back includes giving of yourself to those you love. I'm learning that sometimes less is more and that I can work smarter to accomplish more in less time. My new byword has become balance. One of my resolutions is to do less – less checking my phone or email after work, less working late and less saying "yes" to things that conflict with family time. Less, in this case, will lead to more memories with my family and allow me to recharge so I can actually be more productive in life and business. Consider joining me in re-prioritizing and doing "less" to achieve more.

GIVING for GROWTH

IT'S NOT TOO LATE

It's hard to believe how quickly time passes. It seems like only yesterday that I was rocking my younger son, as a baby, to sleep in my arms. Well, my older son is now 14; and my younger son will soon turn 9. With each passing day, I am taking more to heart these pearls of wisdom: "Life is short!" and "Enjoy every moment because your kids grow up quickly!" Indeed, there is nothing more precious than time!

This being said, time can work in your favor, regardless of your age. Although we can't fully control the length of time we have on Earth, we can control how we use our time and where we set our focus. Society tends to prioritize and glamourize wealth and accumulation; but few people ever recall the size of our bank accounts or homes after we're gone. What will long be remembered – and cherished – is how much we loved, uplifted, and enhanced the lives of others. I'll say it again, the length of our life is a blessing; but the quality of our life is our legacy.

The good news for all workaholics is that it's not too late to reprioritize your life! Take note of what good came from this for Alfred Nobel. It was through the directives of his last will that he established the Nobel Prize, which has, since 1901, been honoring men and women from around the world for outstanding achievements in physics, chemistry, physiology or medicine, literature, and for work in peace. Interestingly, the creation of this venerable award was a result of an unintended error (or perhaps divine intervention).

When Alfred's brother, Ludvig, died, a newspaper mistakenly ran the obituary of Alfred Nobel, believing that it was he who had passed away. Because Alfred Nobel was known as the inventor of dynamite, the newspaper chose a most unflattering headline to announce his demise: "The merchant of death is dead." The article went on to say, "Dr. Alfred Nobel, who became rich by finding ways to kill more people faster than ever before, died yesterday." Alfred Nobel was horrified by this assessment of his life. He decided it was not the legacy he wanted to leave; so he dedicated his fortune to honoring and rewarding those who benefited mankind. As a result, the Nobel Prize today stands as one of the most famous and prestigious humanitarian awards.

What will your legacy be? If the life you're living today is not the epitaph you want permanently inscribed on your headstone, you have the power to rewrite it. Act now; and take those three daily steps toward transforming your life into one of giving back to others. As Winston Churchill once stated, "We make a living by what we get, but we make a life by what we give." Let's take control and make this the life we want by putting the priority on giving, so we can give our very best and our all to our loved ones, careers, and community!

GIVING for GROWTH

THOUGHTS & ACTION STEPS

POSTLUDE

The road to lights is long, yet still I press on
because I'm not giving up on my dream.
I've never given up on anything!
I can see the taillights in front
and I can see the headlights behind,
but it doesn't matter…this dream is mine.

I wrote this poem when I was a junior at the University of North Texas, as a reminder that realizing my dream of moving to Los Angeles and pursuing a career in the entertainment industry wasn't going to be easy. It would mean moving 1,400 miles away from my support network in Texas to a city with more than 10 million people competing for opportunities; a city where I knew no one.

To succeed, I knew it would take personal sacrifice, hard work, and dedication. My road map for staying on course was basic. I resolved to do three things each day to make "progress." This could be something as simple as meeting someone new, practicing my craft, or working on the lyrics to a song.

Just as important, my road map required staying true to my values and myself. All too often, as people are navigating the road of life, they become so fixated on the taillights ahead of them that they lose sight of their own destination. It's easy to become distracted by chasing the taillights, comparing vehicles or how fast others are driving. There will always be those who have more, are further ahead in their careers, have more physical ability, and so on; but dreams are personal. Don't be a distracted driver! Remember that each person's path is different; each dream is as unique as its individual creator. It's in the pursuit of our dreams that we find happiness; and it's in the attainment of our dreams that we achieve success.

I was blessed to fulfill my dreams in Los Angeles and to make friends whom I now consider family. I'm now working on a new set of dreams here in the Mid-South with my wife and children. As with my family, my hope for us all is that we strive to support each other in dreaming BIG and to being committed to doing three things each day in order to bring our dreams to fruition. Let us not get distracted comparing "things" when we can expend that energy lifting up and helping others realize their dreams, too. I can think of no better legacy to leave!

I truly hope you enjoyed this book and found some helpful tips that will empower you to realize your own dreams, become more engaged in your community and make a difference in the lives of others. After all, that's what life should be all about...helping others!

You can help me keep new ideas coming and the Giving for Growth momentum going in the following ways: 1) Visit our website at **cityCURRENT.com**; 2) Email me at **JCP@cityCURRENT.com**; 3) Join the conversation on social media using **@jeremycpark** and **@cityCURRENT**; 4) Use #PowertheGOOD to share your ideas and giving back in action. Together we can make a difference... three daily steps at a time!

ACKNOWLEDGEMENTS

Nothing great is ever accomplished alone. Behind every person's "success" is a support team that encompasses the myriad family members, friends, mentors, co-workers, and others who have lent a helping hand to that individual along his or her journey. The person who has visually attained the success may receive individual accolades for the achievement; but the truth is life is the ultimate team sport! With each victory on the court, in the classroom, or in the boardroom, there is always more than that ONE person who has invested his or her time, energy, talents, and efforts in reaching that goal. This book is truly a testament to the power of teamwork and to the countless individuals who have so generously blessed me with their support, friendship, love, and trust.

For my family and me, God is the guiding light; we rely on His amazing grace and infinite wisdom to illuminate the course we should navigate for our lives. I truly believe that my mission in life, as well as in our work with cityCURRENT, is to help others and to improve our community and our society. So, whenever we talk about making a difference, my personal purpose is rooted in faith and family.

I'm abundantly blessed with a stunningly beautiful, superhero wife, Meredith, and two precious boys, Cooper and Cayson. They're my pride and joy and my source of support and inspiration. Meredith is my saving grace! I live life at warp speed; but she calmly slows me down so I can enjoy the journey.

Meredith is busy with her own full-time career; yet she always successfully manages to keep the Park household running smoothly. What good I achieve in life, indeed, is a direct result of the love and support of Meredith and our boys!

My parents, Julie and John Park, continue to be positive influences in my life, as well. During my childhood and youth, they made volunteering a top priority in our family life; and they encouraged my younger brother and me to be involved in programs centered on community service, like the Boy Scouts of America.

My brother, Jeff, earned the rank of Eagle Scout and proudly serves our country as a U.S. Marine. He is an incredible role model for giving back! (During one of his multiple tours of combat duty, Jeff earned the Bronze Star with valor. He'll never mention this himself, though.) Jeff's life has been blessed with an adorable son, Thomas, a beautiful girl, Harper, and an amazing wife, Rachel, who has gracefully accepted the countless, untold sacrifices that are inherent with being a military family. I'm always humbled by and grateful for each and every one of my brother's and his family's sacrifices – and of the similar sacrifices made by all those who serve in the military and as first responders, as well as their families. Their selfless acts of giving allow all of us in America to live freely so we can follow our dreams!

It's fitting that I acknowledge the members of my extended family, which includes the Flemings, the Moores, and the Conroys. I also acknowledge the members of my wife's family: Wallace Crumby (grandfather), John Hussey (father), Alesha and Preston Knight (sister and brother-in-law), and Jennifer and Brett Garrett (sister and brother-in-law) – along with all the nieces, nephews, and cousins on both sides of our family. A heartfelt word of thanks is sent "upward" to these beloved family members we have lost, but not forgotten: my aunt and uncle, Diane and Tommy Park; my uncle, Roger Conroy, Sr; my grandfather, Frank Ivers; Meredith's mother, Kay Hussey; and Meredith's grandmother, Inez Crumby. I am immeasurably blessed being embraced by so many compassionate and loving family members, who care deeply about me, my family, others, and our country.

This book and ALL the good that has and will come from cityCURRENT's activities are the direct results of the combined efforts of my truly remarkable, dedicated co-workers at Lipscomb & Pitts Insurance and our cityCURRENT partners, who have selflessly given of their time and resources to accomplish our common philanthropic goals. We could not have achieved such an extraordinary level of success, however, had we not had the loyal support of the countless friends we interact with across the Mid-South and throughout our nation, as well. This support system includes all the business, nonprofit, education, government, and faith professionals and leaders, who are, themselves, doing so much good. You all are my friends and mentors; and each of you inspires me daily to push the boundaries, challenge the status quo, and find new ways to raise the bar of excellence together. I love that we're rolling up our sleeves and working to help others; and I'm proud of the positive impact we're making as a team!

Speaking of team, I am forever indebted to Johnny Pitts, who believed in me from the start and gave me the freedom and support to forge a philanthropic path for our organization. It's an honor and a privilege working with Johnny, Mat Lipscomb III, Lipscomb & Pitts Insurance, and cityCURRENT. We dreamed BIG; but we could never have foreseen how far our dream of becoming a catalyst for our community would take us! We've exceeded all our original expectations – and, yet, the best is still to come!

My co-workers and cityCURRENT teammates, Allison Carson and Andrew Bartolotta, deserve recognition. They work tirelessly to help organize and execute all of our events and efforts, manage our website, produce and curate our media, and push the boundaries of what's possible. CJ Kirkland and our other longtime freelance journalists, including Stacey and Lance Wiedower, are "rock stars," too. They are masterful storytellers, who are playing key roles in not only sharing the good taking place in the Mid-South, but taking our organization to new heights, as well. They all deserve kudos for their hard work and efforts!

I offer my appreciation to James Overstreet, who, in 2009, presented me with the idea of writing a weekly column focused on sharing philanthropic ideas and spotlighting nonprofits. My "Giving Back" column officially launched in 2010 and I've been pleased that, over these many years, we've been able to highlight hundreds of organizations and individuals who are making a difference; and we've shared innumerable helpful tips to increase community engagement and to make philanthropy and volunteerism easy and fun.

George Cogswell, retired Publisher of The Commercial Appeal, and Paul Jewell, who retired after thirty-nine years at the media company, are two other people deserving recognition. I thank them for sharing the vision and for supporting both cityCURRENT and my "Giving Back" column. It has been a tremendous honor having the column published each Sunday in The Commercial Appeal; and I'm grateful for the opportunity. Working with The Commercial Appeal team has been a real pleasure and I'm excited to continue celebrating the good taking place here in the Mid-South and working to inspire even more people to become catalysts in our community.

My gratitude is offered, as well, to Jonathan Lindberg and his team at Main Street Books. Jonathan turned my first book, *Giving Back with Purpose: Fueling Growth through Community Involvement* into a reality in 2013. All proceeds from that book have benefited youth-serving literacy programs in the Mid-South; and thanks to readers, just like you, we've been able to contribute many thousands of dollars to organizations, such as Binghampton Christian Academy, Shelby County Books from Birth, and the Community Foundation of Northwest Mississippi. It was exciting publishing a book about giving back, which is literally giving back. And, now we're doing the same with this second book! I applaud Jonathan and his team for all their hard work and for bringing both my literary works to life. Jonathan's vision and support made the process of writing a book fun and easy, and for that, I am immensely grateful.

In closing, I thank all of my good friends like Anthony Cava and Brian Leinbach, who are like brothers; and each of the mentors, coaches, and teachers who've guided me along the way. Entertainment icons Merv Griffin, Dick Clark, and Cindy Clark deserve recognition, too, because they helped shape my perspectives on media and opened doors of opportunities that led me to where I am today. My final "thank you" is, once again, directed to my family and all of our partners and friends with cityCURRENT, who truly make everything we do possible! My life and our efforts are the bright reflections of your combined talents, wisdom, generosity, and love. Always remember I highly value each of you and deeply appreciate everything you have done and continue to do for me and for our community!

GIVING for GROWTH